THE RESTORATION AND THE ENGLAND OF CHARLES II

The Restoration and the England of Charles II
SECOND EDITION

JOHN MILLER

LONGMAN
LONDON AND NEW YORK

Addison Wesley Longman Limited
Edinburgh Gate
Harlow, Essex CM20 2JE
England
and Associated Companies throughout the world

Published in the United States of America
by Addison Wesley Longman Inc., New York

First published 1985
Second edition 1997

ISBN 0 582 292239 Paper

British Library Cataloguing-in-Publication Data

A catalogue record for this book is available from the British Library

Library of Congress Cataloging-in-Publication Data

Miller, John, 1946–
    The restoration and the England of Charles II / John Miller. --
2nd ed.
        p. cm.
    Originally published: London: New York: Longman, 1985, in
series: Seminar studies in history.
    Includes bibliographical references (p.) and index.
    Summary: Chronicles the twenty-five year reign of Charles II under whose rule
Parliament kept most of the powers it had won under Cromwell and shared
governing authority with the king.
    ISBN 0-582-29223-9 (paper: alk. paper)
    1. Great Britain--History--Charles II, 1660–1685. 2. Great Britain--Politics
and government--1660–1688. [1. Great Britain--History--Charles II, 1660–1685.
2. Great Britain--Politics and government--1660–1688.] I. Title.
DA445.M45 1997
941.06'6--DC21   96-50299
                                                                           CIP
                                                                            AC

Set by 7 in 10/12 Sabon
Produced through Longman Malaysia, PP

CONTENTS

AN INTRODUCTION TO THE SERIES

Such is the pace of historical enquiry in the modern world that there is an ever-widening gap between the specialist article or monograph, incorporating the results of current research, and general surveys, which inevitably become out of date. *Seminar Studies in History* are designed to bridge this gap. The series was founded by Patrick Richardson in 1966 and his aim was to cover major themes in British, European and World history. Between 1980 and 1996 Roger Lockyer continued his work, before handing the editorship over to Clive Emsley and Gordon Martel. Clive Emsley is Professor of History at the Open University, while Gordon Martel is Professor of International History at the University of Northern British Columbia, Canada and Senior Research Fellow at De Montfort University.

All the books are written by experts in their field who are not only familiar with the latest research but have often contributed to it. They are frequently revised, in order to take account of new information and interpretations. They provide a selection of documents to illustrate major themes and provoke discussion, and also a guide to further reading. The aim of *Seminar Studies* is to clarify complex issues without over-simplifying them, and to stimulate readers into deepening their knowledge and understanding of major themes and topics.

PREFACE TO THE SECOND EDITION

When I wrote the preface to the first edition, in 1983, I remarked that the reign of Charles II had been less intensively studied than the two decades which immediately preceded it. For many years, the most important task facing seventeenth-century historians had seemed to be finding the causes of the civil war. This had the effect of turning attention to before 1640 and of detaching the history of Restoration England from that of the first sixty years of the century. For many historians, the collapse of the restored monarchy in 1688 confirmed that the civil wars and their aftermath had brought about a permanent shift in the balance of power between king and Parliament (or people), which implied that the Restoration period was of little intrinsic interest or importance.

I am pleased to say that work published in the last fifteen to twenty years has done much to remove the imbalance which stemmed from an over-concentration on the mid-century decades. We now have a much fuller and more sophisticated understanding of early Stuart government and politics, while a number of younger scholars are asking new and searching questions of the Restoration period. The work of Mark Goldie, Tim Harris, Ronald Hutton, Mark Knights, Steve Pincus, Jonathan Scott, Paul Seaward and John Spurr (to name but a few) has stimulated lively debate on a variety of topics, including the relationship between religion and politics, the nature and meaning of 'party', the extent of popular involvement in politics and the extent to which 'opinion' can be measured. Meanwhile, scholars like Andrew Coleby and Stephen Roberts have begun to undertake the sort of local studies which did so much to qualify (if not discredit) some of the more brash assertions about the nature of the mid-century crisis. Whereas I regretted in 1983 that there was no good general study of the Restoration settlement, there are now two [79; 116]. Last but not least, several of the above-named have sought to place the Restoration period in a longer historical perspective, to link it up with the period before 1660 and to assess the impact of the experience of civil war on the next generation.

I divided the first edition into two parts: a comparatively detailed discussion of the Restoration settlement, in the context of what had gone before, and a much more general discussion of the way the settlement worked out during the remainder of the reign. I decided to concentrate on England: although there was inevitably interaction between England, Scotland and Ireland in this period, I do not feel that it was as dramatic or significant as in 1637–51 or 1688–91. I have followed the same basic format for the new edition. The fact that such a wide range of material has appeared since 1983 has necessitated a broad rewrite, but there have been particularly substantial additions on the constitution, the nature of political divisions and taxation and the growth of the state. Inevitably, much has had to be omitted or compressed, but what remains is intended to serve as an introduction to the increasingly rich and complex literature on this important period.

NOTE ON REFERENCING SYSTEM

Readers should note that numbers in square brackets [5] refer them to the corresponding entry in the Bibliography at the end of the book (specific page numbers are given in italics). A number in square brackets preceded by *Doc.* [*Doc.* 5] refers readers to the corresponding item in the Documents section which follows the main text. Words which are defined in the Glossary are asterisked on their first occurrence in the book.

ACKNOWLEDGEMENTS

The publishers would like to thank the following for permission to reproduce copyright material:

Cambridge University Press for extracts taken from *English Historical Documents 1660–1714*, edited by A. Browning published in 1953; 'The Whig Theory of the Constitution in the Reign of Charles II' quoted in B. Behrens, *Cambridge Historical Journal* published in 1941; an extract from *Science and Social Welfare in the Age of Newton,* by G.N. Clark published in 1949 by permission of Oxford University Press; The Royal Historical Society for an extract from 'The Diurnal of Thomas Rugg, 1659–1661' edited by W.L. Sachse published in 1961; Humphrey Salway for an extract from The Diary of Seymour Bowman MP.

PART ONE: THE RESTORATION

1 THE END OF THE INTERREGNUM

It might seem odd that Charles II's return to England in 1660 was greeted with almost universal rejoicing. His father, Charles I, had been defeated in a bloody civil war, and executed; Charles had spent years in apparently hopeless exile. If the Parliamentarians* had set out to destroy the monarchy, its subsequent restoration would indeed have been extraordinary, but most had not. In the 1640s the great majority of the ruling elite wished to preserve the 'ancient constitution',* with its. balance between the powers of the Crown and the rights of the subject, its stress on taxation by consent and the rule of law.

They saw that constitution as under threat, from two directions. First, Charles I failed to govern in a way that his subjects regarded as fair and reasonable. After 1629 he ruled without Parliament, the traditional embodiment of government by consent. He stretched his fiscal rights to the limit in a way which might just be within the letter of the law, but was contrary to its spirit. Along with fiscal rapacity and chicanery went an authoritarian style of government. The JPs* who directed local government had traditionally, and wisely, been allowed a measure of discretion, adapting national regulations to suit local circumstances. Charles demanded that JPs carry out their instructions to the letter and added insult to injury by involving them in his unpopular fiscal expedients. Finally, his regime was increasingly tainted with 'Popery'. Archbishop Laud's emphasis on ritual and ceremony led to accusations that he was leading the Church of England back to Catholicism. Even more sinister was the influence at court of Catholics such as the Queen, Henrietta Maria.

By 1640 it was widely believed that Charles, or those about him, wished to establish Catholicism and absolutism.* A Scots invasion forced him to call what became known as the Long Parliament and to abandon some of the institutions and most of the fiscal devices abused in the 1630s, but, despite his concessions, Charles failed to regain his subjects' trust because of repeated indications that he wished to use force to reverse them. Fear of bloody reprisals and arbitrary rule drove many moderates to go beyond the remedying of past grievances and to endorse novel demands, notably that Parliament should share in the king's control of the armed forces and in his choice of advisers. In so doing, they were driven less by a desire for constitutional change than by a simple concern for self-preservation: to reduce the king's power to a point where he would be unable to harm his subjects.

If the misuse of royal power posed one possible threat to the 'ancient constitution', another emerged after the Long Parliament met. Some MPs denounced the attempts to restrict the king's powers as novel and illegal. When the king and Lords resisted measures which the Commons' leaders saw as vital, the latter appealed to a wider public outside Parliament. The dramatic events of 1640–41 and the collapse of press censorship stimulated an explosion of popular political debate. Londoners, fearful of the Papists and the king's soldiers, took to the streets, striking fear into the king and peers; there were widespread disorders in the provinces directed against Catholics, altar rails and unpopular landlords. The collapse of the bishops' authority allowed people to discuss religion and to worship as they wished. To many of the ruling elite, established authority in Church, state and society was threatened by the brute power of the 'many-headed monster', the mob. If fear of absolutism led many conservative gentlemen to side with Parliament, fear of anarchy drove many others to support the king. 'The alteration of government,' wrote the Earl of Northumberland, 'is apprehended on both sides' [137 *p. 414*].

At first, the majority in Parliament hoped that, if they could avoid defeat, Charles would have to negotiate. When it became clear that he would not do so, they were forced to adopt a more aggressive approach. The Solemn League and Covenant* of 1643 secured military help from the Scots, but at the price of a commitment to abolish bishops and to introduce some form of Presbyterianism.* Meanwhile, the war imposed a great burden on the people. Taxes were far heavier than ever before; both sides' local agents acted arbitrarily when mobilising men and munitions; the armies requisitioned, plundered and disrupted normal economic activity. By 1646 much of the popular support which Parliament enjoyed in 1642 had evaporated and the demand grew to end war taxation, disband the armies and return to normal.

That, however, required a settlement with the king, and he refused to make meaningful concessions. In the resultant stalemate Parliament's most successful army, the New Model, turned on its creator. Angered by what it saw as Parliament's ingratitude and the populace's unreasonable hostility, the army formulated its own political demands, which included freedom of worship for the growing number of sectarian congregations (or gathered churches) which had mushroomed since 1640. After the army marched on London in August 1647, it was apparent that no force in the country could stand against it. Its leaders subjected the Houses to increasing pressure, especially after Charles deliberately renewed hostilities in the Second Civil War in 1648. Convinced that the king had to go, the army demanded that Parliament break off negotiations with him. It refused, so on 6 December 1648 Colonel Pride arrested those MPs most in favour of negotiation and turned others away. Many more refused to take their seats, in protest. The remaining minority, or 'Rump', set up a high court of justice which tried and condemned the king: he was executed on 30 January 1649. Some weeks later the monarchy was abolished, along with the House of Lords, almost all the peers having withdrawn. England was declared a 'commonwealth or free state'.

Pride's Purge and Charles's execution were the pivotal events of the 'English Revolution'. They removed all hope of a negotiated settlement based on the traditional constitution and ensured that the regimes of the 1650s would be dependent on the army. The Parliamentarians of the 1640s had been divided, but the Long Parliament had been legally convened and represented a large part of the nation. After Pride's Purge any claim to continuity or constitutionality became a tenuous fiction. The Rump might talk of the sovereignty of the people and pose as the ongoing incarnation of the Long Parliament and the people's representative, but it was well aware of its lack of support. Pride's Purge and Charles's execution were carried through by a small, unrepresentative minority. Most Parliamentarians (not to mention Royalists) abhorred both. The driving force behind them was the army, self-consciously separate from (and, in its own eyes, morally superior to) civilian society, a 'godly remnant', an instrument raised up by God to do His will. Militarily it was invulnerable: by 1651 it had crushed the remaining opposition within the British Isles, while a greatly expanded navy guarded the republic against foreign attack. Its civilian allies, however, were few and disunited.

The Commonwealth and its successor regime, the Protectorate (headed from 1653–8 by Oliver Cromwell) rested heavily on military force, but should not be seen simply as a military dictatorship [136]. Cromwell resisted the call of some of his officers to impose a 'dictatorship of the godly', seeking instead to heal the divisions of civil war by broadening the regime's civilian support. This aspiration rested in part on a principled commitment to Parliaments, although this never prevented him from using force against them if it seemed necessary (as when he turned out the Rump in 1653). It was also pragmatic. Large though the New Model was, it was too small to impose its will by force on the whole of the British Isles. In particular, the soldiers' pay (and therefore morale) depended on taxpayers' continued willingness to pay and that in turn depended on taxation being held down to a bearable level and on a sense (on the part of the taxpayers) that the taxes were legitimate – in other words, that they had been voted by some sort of Parliament. That sense of legitimacy would be further enhanced if the public perceived that the regime was actively seeking consent. Such considerations limited the fiscal options of the regimes of the 1650s. At first, they were tided over by the sale of lands confiscated from the Crown, the Church and the Royalists, but once those had gone they were dependent on taxation. In the later 1650s the Protectorate reduced taxes in order to try to buy support, which drew the regime into a downward spiral of debt which in turn reduced its capacity to borrow [39; 49]. But the alternative, relying on naked military force, did not work either, as became apparent in 1659.

The traditional mechanism for securing support was Parliament, but to secure an amenable Parliament was not easy. The republic had some support among political and religious radicals, but these lacked both numbers and political weight. Those who counted politically were the landed elite (nobility and gentry) and the leading citizens of the towns, who would dominate any electoral system, thanks to their power as landlords, employers and consumers and the respect in which they were held by those lower down the social scale. Only a tiny minority of this elite wholeheartedly supported the regimes of the 1650s. The Royalists were irreconcilable, so the obvious source of support was from among the Parliamentarians, notably those moderates, usually known as Presbyterians, who had been alienated by Pride's Purge and the king's execution.

Unfortunately for Cromwell, the Presbyterians' views differed markedly from his. First, he was committed to religious liberty. He preserved the outward structure of a national Church, with a minister in each parish supported by tithes,* but allowed the clergy a wide latitude in matters of worship and doctrine. Those who wished to worship elsewhere could do so, except for Papists or 'prelatists' (supporters of the old episcopal Church and Prayer Book). The Presbyterians believed in a single, fairly uniform Church to which all should belong. This they saw as essential if moral discipline and theological orthodoxy were to be maintained. Secondly, Cromwell wished to preserve the army (not least as the guarantor of religious liberty); the Presbyterians thought it expensive, tyrannical and unacceptably radical, and longed to be rid of it. Thirdly, Cromwell (and the army) were committed to the republic. The Presbyterians believed in monarchy, preferably a Stuart monarchy. Such fundamental differences made long-term co-operation unlikely, unless Cromwell abandoned the army and ruled as the Presbyterians wanted. Many Presbyterians served in local government and sought election to Cromwell's Parliaments, but often did so merely in order to change or undermine his regime from within. Cromwell could work with his Parliaments only by circumscribing their powers and imposing political conditions on their members. When such restrictions were removed, in 1658, chaos ensued.

Cromwell's problem was simple: 'I am as much for a government by consent as any man, but where shall we find that consent?' [19 II, *p. 11*]. (He should have added that he wanted consent on his own terms.) His reliance on the military was most apparent when his concern for security overrode his wish for consent. The rule of the Major-Generals, in 1655–6, came as a rude shock to Parliamentarian squires who, since 1653, had begun to take part in local government again. Outsiders with a stern sense of duty, the Major-Generals and their subordinates had little time for the favouritism and tempering of national requirements to local conditions which were a traditional feature of local government. 'Was I made a commissioner to do good or favour to my friends?' asked one officer. 'I never thought so, but to serve the state' [34 *p. 175*]. Such a centralised, authoritarian approach to government made that of the 1630s appear mild in retrospect. Royalists and Presbyterians began to meet socially again and worked together in elections; Presbyterians corresponded with the exiled Charles II [34 Ch. 7].

Politically isolated, the army retained its unity after Cromwell's death, on 3 September 1658. His son, Richard, who succeeded him as Lord Protector, was a civilian and many Presbyterians hoped that his regime would be less dependent on the army. He called a

Parliament early in 1659 which tried to restrict religious toleration and establish civilian control over the military. The army retaliated by forcing Richard to stand down and recalled the Rump. The Rump's dismissal in 1653 still rankled, but it needed the army's military strength to make up for its own lack of support. The army needed the Rump to cover the nakedness of military rule with a cloak of spurious legitimacy and, above all, to vote taxes. Their relationship was thus less than harmonious and the final break came on the issue of which was the dominant partner. The Rump insisted that it should control military appointments and promotions, the army's council of war disagreed, and on 13 October the Rump was expelled for the second time.

England thus reverted to direct military rule, but the committee of safety set up by the army faced great problems. The last of the taxes voted by the Rump would expire in December and there were many reports of refusals to pay taxes not voted by Parliament. (Even Oliver had been reluctant to allow the legality of the Protectorate's taxes to be tested in the courts [39].) The committee soon abandoned its threats to quarter soldiers on recalcitrant taxpayers, realising that this could provoke a general revolt. The City, restive and hostile, rejected requests for a loan. The judges refused to hear any more cases. Government was in danger of grinding to a halt and the regime was constantly reminded of its unpopularity. It tried to strengthen its support by creating a militia of 'sectaries' (Baptists and Quakers), but this merely increased resentment and did not solve the basic problem of the need for a more permanent form of government. It was announced that a free government would be set up that was acceptable to all, but without a king or House of Lords, which for most was a contradiction in terms. By December it seemed that England was sliding into confusion.

The army leaders' problems were compounded by the conduct of General George Monk, an experienced professional soldier who commanded the army in Scotland. His competence as a soldier and military administrator is beyond doubt [*Doc. 1*], but opinions varied as to his political abilities and the motives behind his conduct in 1659–60. Naturally, after the Restoration, he and his biographers [13; 25] claimed that he had intended, from the outset, to bring back the king, which would imply a political farsightedness of which there was later little sign: Pepys called him a blockhead. Indeed, if that was Monk's intention, it was far from obvious at the time: 'He is a black Monk and I cannot see through him,' wrote one Royalist [6 III, *p. 651*].

Many were confused by his capacity for saying one thing and doing another. It seems likely that he was trying to keep his options open and to cover himself against charges of acting without authority. Having served both king and republic, he probably lacked dogmatic attachment to any form of government, although he consistently stressed the need for order and authority in Church and state. He was considering restoring the king in the summer of 1659. He wrote to Sir Anthony Ashley Cooper, a Presbyterian who had accepted office under Cromwell, that he wanted the Long Parliament recalled – in other words, with a Presbyterian majority, as it had been before Pride's Purge reduced it to a Rump. He was in contact with Royalist emissaries at the time of the rising in July–August 1659 of Sir George Booth – a former Parliamentarian, who had considerable Royalist support – and might have joined it had it not been defeated so quickly. Contacts with Presbyterians, Royalists and Rumpers continued in the autumn. A group of Presbyterian politicians, including the Earl of Manchester, tried to persuade him to bring back Charles II on the conditions offered to his father on the Isle of Wight in 1648, including stringent restrictions on the prerogative and a Presbyterian system of Church government. (Insofar as Monk expressed any views on religion, it would seem that he was a Presbyterian.)

Monk was stirred to political action by the growing confusion in England and by the interference of first the Rump, then the army leaders, in military appointments in Scotland. The Rump's expulsion gave him a pretext to take his stand on a defence of legally constituted authority and the superiority of the civil to the military power – especially as the Rump's council of state secretly sent him a commission as commander-in-chief of the entire army. He declared for a civilian government without king or Lords and for a settled godly ministry, began to purge his forces of officers whose loyalty was suspect, and prepared to march into England.

As Monk's preparations would take time, he embarked on tortuous negotiations with the English army leaders. News of his activities gave heart to opponents of army rule, especially in London. Late in November he wrote to the lord mayor and common council, asking for their help in restoring Parliament to its former freedom – whether he meant the Rump or the Parliament of 1648 was unclear [9; 23]. The City authorities responded warily, but the letter gave added force to the demand in London for a 'free Parliament' – perhaps a new, freely elected body, perhaps that of 1648. (Either would probably recall the king.)

Many soldiers in the English army also looked to Monk, whose men were paid more regularly than they were. Some were confused by the divisions among their leaders and 'laid down their arms till they be satisfied for what and whom they engage' [9 *p. 211*]. 'The soldiers here [London],' said a newsletter, 'are so vilified, scorned and hissed that they are ashamed to march' [9 *p. 166*].

Caught between the citizens and the army, the City authorities side-stepped demands that they should petition for a free Parliament. The committee of safety fulminated that to promote such a petition was treason and bleated that Monk would bring back the king. It announced that a new Parliament (with tightly restricted powers) would meet on 24 January, but it was too late. Portsmouth's garrison declared for the Rump, as did a section of the fleet, which blockaded the Thames. In the London common council elections, the army's allies were heavily defeated. The new common council called for a 'free Parliament' (although it could not agree what that meant) and demanded that the City should again organise its own militia, in place of the militia of 'sectaries' which the army had tried to create. As the army's resolve crumbled, the Rump reconvened on 26 December and Major-General Fleetwood said sadly that God had spat in his face.

The Rump proved as arrogant and vindictive as ever. Having voted the soldiers a month's pay, to keep them quiet, it began a purge of officers who had supported the committee of safety. It refused to admit some twenty-five MPs 'secluded' at Pride's Purge, unless they subscribed to the Engagement* (against government by a king or House of Lords); they refused. It revived an earlier plan to fill 'vacant' seats (including those of 'secluded' MPs) by holding elections, with stringent conditions to ensure that those elected would be politically acceptable to the Rumpers.

Despite its bravado, the Rump remained politically weak. It appointed a council of state to direct the government, but fewer than half its members would take the Engagement. Calls for a free Parliament continued: both Royalists and Presbyterians saw this as the first step towards restoring the monarchy, even if they differed as to the terms on which it should be restored. Both had had their confidence boosted in December and had established a strong position in the City's government and militia, but fear of the army made the City's rulers reluctant to take a political stand. Everything depended on Monk [*Doc. 2*] who on 1 January 1660 marched into England.

As he headed south he was assailed from all sides with petitions, importunities and advice. Presbyterian peers and the City government sent emissaries, Royalists cultivated officers believed to be in his confidence, country gentry urged him to declare for a full, free Parliament, adding that they would pay no taxes until such a Parliament was called [*Doc. 3*]. The Rump issued a declaration which tried to reconcile Monk's publicly stated concern for 'magistracy and ministry' with its desire to hang on to power [*Doc. 4*]. Monk talked publicly of his unqualified support for the Rump, from which he derived his authority; some who spoke privately to him believed he sympathised with the call for a free Parliament, but the Rump believed that he would do as he was told. Only his refusal to take the Engagement and his advice to the Rump to hasten the elections it promised, without increasing the restrictions on future MPs, hinted at some disquiet on his part.

His loyalty to the Rump was soon put to the test. On 8 February the City common council resolved to pay no taxes until London's full complement of MPs was restored. The Rump ordered Monk to take down the City's gates and the posts and chains across the streets and voted that the common council should be 'discontinued'. Monk had the posts and chains removed, but not the gates, saying that he was sure that the common council would rescind its vote if allowed to meet. The Rump was adamant: the gates were to be destroyed and a new common council elected, on a basis laid down by Parliament. It also resolved that the army should be governed by five commissioners, including Monk, of whom three should be a quorum. Hitherto, Monk had acted by virtue of his commission as sole commander-in-chief, granted by the Rump's previous council of state. Now he could be outvoted by the other commissioners.

It was the last straw. Already unhappy about the orders given him, he demanded that the Rump should proceed at once to fill vacancies by fresh elections; whereas the Rump had stipulated that (in effect) only republicans should be eligible, Monk insisted that membership should be open to all who had supported Parliament in the civil wars. This would ensure a moderate or Presbyterian majority: the few sitting republicans would be outnumbered by newly-elected moderates.

Ten days of complex manoeuvres followed. Monk remained in the City, despite the Rump's pleas that he return to Whitehall. The Rump continued to insist on qualifications which would debar the majority of Parliamentarians from participating in the forthcoming elections. Monk therefore opted for another method of filling up the Rump with moderates. On 21 February, guarded by Monk's troops, the MPs excluded in 1648 took their seats. Monk urged the enlarged Parliament to provide for a speedy dissolution and fresh elections for a new Parliament which, he said, 'may meet and act in freedom, for the more full establishing of this commonwealth, without a king, single person or House of Lords' [23 XXII, *p. 143*].

In the following weeks Monk became more inscrutable than ever, but his actions tended towards establishing a succession of Presbyterian Parliaments, which implied the restoration of the king, but on stringent conditions. When he asked Parliament, now with a Presbyterian majority, to settle 'such qualifications as may secure the public cause we are all engaged in,' he must have expected these to exclude Royalists, at least for the time being, from voting or entering Parliament: that, certainly, is what happened. Parliament appointed a council of state, dominated by Presbyterians such as Ashley Cooper, Annesley and Holles, which sought to re-establish the short-lived Presbyterian Church system of the 1640s (which had never won much support).

Monk was well aware that these moves would be deeply resented by the many republicans and religious radicals in the army. On the day the secluded MPs were restored, Monk and his officers issued a declaration in which they tried to assure the army that they would not betray all that it had fought for [*Doc. 5*]. Monk also began a lengthy purge of the officer corps of the army and navy, while Parliament sought to create an alternative military force, a new militia commanded by Presbyterian, and sometimes Royalist, gentry. Monk dealt firmly with criticism of his conduct from within the army and demanded that the officers, and later the soldiers, should promise to submit to whatever should be decided by the next Parliament [7].

By the time Parliament dissolved itself on 16 March the question was not whether the king would be restored, but on what terms. The outgoing Parliament did all it could to ensure that those terms would favour the Presbyterians. The qualifications laid down for MPs excluded both Royalists and 'such persons that deny magistracy or ministry . . . to be the ordinances of God' [10 VII, *p. 874*]. If observed, these provisions would have ensured a Presbyterian majority, but public opinion moved so strongly in favour of monarchy that many Royalists were elected [71].

Monk's role remained crucial, because he alone could control the army. As always, he moved cautiously, partly to avoid outraging the army (which was still being purged), partly because he wished to see how the elections turned out. Late in March he at last agreed to receive overtures from the king and opposed those Presbyterians on the council of state who sought to prescribe conditions for the king's return before Parliament met. As the election results showed the strength of Royalism and Monk refused to endorse their proposals, individual Presbyterians began to make their peace with the king and to seek office.

They found an unlikely ally. Henrietta Maria had done much to bring about her husband's downfall and now sought to gain an ascendancy over her son. Both the Presbyterians and the Queen Mother's English followers hoped to supplant some of Charles I's old servants – Edward Hyde, Edward Nicholas and the Marquis of Ormond – who were currently prominent at Charles II's court. Together with the French ambassador in London, they schemed to persuade Charles to go from Brussels to Paris, where his mother could preside over the negotiations for his return. As a Catholic, she had no qualms about making concessions at the expense of the Church of England, or of the prerogative, provided these enabled her to exclude Hyde and his friends from power and establish her influence over her son.

Their intrigues bore little fruit. Charles moved not to France but to Breda. In mid-April the French ambassador wrote that only Monk could prevent an unconditional restoration. As Monk refused to insist on the qualifications drawn up by the previous Parliament, those of Royalist antecedents elected to the Commons were able to remain, denying the Presbyterians their expected majority. They tried instead to exclude Royalists from the Lords on various pretexts and hoped to use their control of the Upper House to determine the terms of the king's return. Again Monk disappointed them, allowing Royalist peers to take their seats.

The Presbyterians' projects collapsed soon after the new Parliament, or 'Convention', met on 25 April. On 1 May the Commons heard the king's Declaration of Breda, which referred to Parliament, the contentious issues of Crown and Church lands, religious toleration and the punishment of the regicides, and promised to pay the army's arrears in full [*Doc. 6*]. It was a shrewd document. It dealt with the points on which individual Parliamentarians and soldiers had most need of reassurance: after all, taking up arms against the king was treason under existing law. It removed fears of indiscriminate royal vengeance, of the arbitrary resumption of Crown and Church lands and of the re-establishment without consultation of the old Church of England. Last, but not least, it held out to the soldiers the prospect of full satisfaction of their professional grievances – above all arrears and indemnity – the denial of which had triggered the army's politicisation in 1647. At the same time, while removing possible barriers to the king's restoration, it left open the question of his powers until after his return.

Early in May the Presbyterians tried several times to impose preconditions on the king. They proposed a committee of both Houses to order the militia and manage affairs of state, on the lines of the Committee of Both Kingdoms of the 1640s. They brought in bills to confirm sales of Crown and Church lands, to grant toleration until a national synod could settle the Church and to grant a general pardon. Monk promoted a package of measures which included some of these and in other ways went further [*Doc. 7*]. Those close to Monk, notably William Morrice, soon to be made Secretary of State, also urged Charles to accept conditions, but he saw no need to do so. There were too many bills before the Houses for any to stand much chance in the face of Royalist obstruction [*Doc. 12*]. Meanwhile, Royalist strength in the provinces became increasingly apparent, as peers and gentry gathered together volunteer troops of horse to counteract the mainly Presbyterian militia – or the still dangerous army.

On 8 May the king was formally proclaimed. As his return was now inevitable, it no longer seemed practical to seek to impose prior conditions, and the ambitious (whether Presbyterian or Royalist) rushed to seek places and favours. The only bills presented to him on his arrival were to confirm the legality of the Convention (in doubt, as it had not been summoned by a king) and of the last eighteen years' judicial proceedings (to prevent a free-for-all in the courts as litigants sought to reverse judgments against them). Other matters could be decided after the king's return.

When Charles landed at Dover on 26 May, and began a triumphal progress to London, England again had a form of government acceptable to the great majority of its people. For more than eleven years its rulers had depended in the last analysis upon military force. Military rule was brought to an end by Monk, who neutralised the army, and by the sheer strength of the popular demand to bring back monarchy. From December 1659 this demand gathered momentum, disconcerted the army grandees, thwarted the Rump and persuaded Monk, probably reluctantly, that an unconditional restoration was unavoidable. When Charles returned, the almost universal rejoicing reflected the national mood [*Docs. 8, 9*]. Time was to show that he could not, or would not, fulfil the manifold and often contradictory expectations which his return aroused. For the moment, however, Royalists and Parliamentarians welcomed him with a degree of unanimity and joy which had not been seen in living memory. As John Evelyn wrote, 'I stood in the Strand, and beheld it, and blessed God' [138 *p. 246*].

2 THE RESTORATION SETTLEMENT: THE CONVENTION

The legislation of 1660–4, which constituted the 'Restoration settlement', was passed by two very different bodies, the Convention of 1660 and the 'Cavalier' Parliament elected early in 1661. Within each there were differences between Commons and Lords and various political and religious interests. Uncertainty abounded: for example, how much of the legislation passed since 1640 should remain in force? So many changes had been carried through by so many different bodies that MPs must have been unsure where to start.

As for the king, he was a stranger to his kingdom, with little first-hand knowledge of its institutions, of his leading subjects and of the relative strengths of the political and religious groups which had fought it out since 1640. He wished to secure his position, but probably had few clear ideas about how to do so and his councillors gave differing advice. Eager to embrace as many shades of opinion as possible, Charles chose sixteen councillors of Royalist backgrounds (most notably Hyde, Nicholas and Ormond), eight Presbyterians (who had opposed Charles I but not co-operated with the republic) and four old Cromwellians, of whom Monk and Ashley Cooper were the most prominent. The varied advice which Charles received ensured that the sporadic acts of Royalist vengeance in the localities were not matched in the policies pursued at national level. There was to be no 'White Terror' in Restoration England [79; 91].

The settlement consisted of a series of *ad hoc* measures, which reflected not only the ebb and flow of politics but also, sometimes, misconceptions on the part of the king or politicians. And yet I shall suggest that the legislation of 1660–4 created a potentially viable basis for a lasting settlement. Piecemeal and untidy though it might be, it reflected a widely felt desire to return to the sort of ordered society and responsible monarchy which should have existed before the civil wars. This chapter and the next will consider the genesis of that legislation.

The Convention is among the most obscure of seventeenth-century Parliaments. It seems to have contained no clear-cut parties, the Commons dividing in different ways on different issues. A substantial proportion – maybe even half – of the Commons were from Parliamentarian backgrounds, but these were not united. Most were Presbyterians – moderates who wanted a Puritan established Church – but a few were radical in politics or wanted a general toleration. Most wanted to restrict Charles's powers, to prevent him from abusing his authority as his father had done, and tried to rush through bills to that effect in the weeks before his return. Some, however, had gained, or sought, office. These resisted attempts to curb the king's authority, either because they needed his favour or because such measures would restrict their own power as the king's servants. Thus Presbyterians like Annesley, Ashley Cooper or Morrice should normally be seen as supporters of the 'court',* working on the king's behalf.

Ranged against the ex-Parliamentarians were many MPs from Royalist backgrounds, elected despite the previous Parliament's efforts to declare them ineligible. By-elections and partisan decisions in election disputes increased their numbers as the year wore on. Despite complaints that these 'young men' did not attend assiduously, except for debates on religion, they were ably led by men like Sir Heneage Finch, while the Presbyterians became divided and disorganised. These MPs' Royalism did not necessarily make them co-operative. They resented what they saw as Charles's undue favour to Presbyterians, which owed something to Monk's influence and to the fear that the Presbyterians might cause trouble if they were not rewarded. They also watched suspiciously for any attempt to accommodate the Presbyterians within the Church of England. The net result of these confused alignments was that on many issues Parliamentarians and Royalists cancelled each other out. The Convention achieved much in areas where there was broad agreement. It settled the most immediate problems left by the Interregnum and took the first steps towards making adequate financial provision for the Crown. On more contentious issues – the prerogative, the militia, the Church – the questions remained open, to be resolved by the Cavalier Parliament.

THE FIRST SESSION

The Convention's proceedings spanned two sessions, with a recess from 13 September to 6 November. The Houses merely adjourned over this period, so that bills unfinished in the first session were carried over to the second, but the nature of the sessions differed. The first was dominated by the legacies of the Interregnum. Matters relating to a long-term settlement were discussed, but had a low priority and major decisions were postponed. The second saw attempts to force decisions on the revenue, the militia and the Church. Meanwhile the political atmosphere at court was changing. In the summer Hyde and other Royalists broadly agreed with the Presbyterian councillors on the need to settle the problems left by the Interregnum, but by the autumn the court was becoming divided on questions of policies and personalities.

The Convention's most immediate problem was the indemnity. Many who had facilitated Charles's return had made war on his father, so were liable to charges of treason. It would also be impossible to disband the army unless its members could be sure of immunity from prosecution for offences committed while in arms. The Declaration of Breda had promised that Charles would assent to a general pardon, but left it to Parliament to decide who should be excluded from its benefits. Some, like Monk, urged that only a handful should forfeit their lives, although others might lose their estates. Many, Presbyterians as well as Royalists, wanted greater severity against both the regicides and the leading figures of the 1650s. Thus the Royalist Job Charlton

> moved against those that petitioned against the king or sat in Parliament between '48 and '49 and the high court of justice men and the contrivers of the Instrument [of Government, which established the Protectorate] and the imposers of taxes under Oliver and major generals and decimators, and though he never pressed for the death of any, yet to secure the future peace of the kingdom he could not be silent. [139 *fo. 49*]

Such measures against those involved in government in the 1650s (including a proposal that they be made to repay their salaries) would penalise men like Monk and Ashley Cooper, who had held office at that time, but not those Presbyterians who had not. Through days of ill-tempered wrangling, MPs gave vent to their vindictiveness while seeking to protect their friends and kinsmen.

The Lords were, if anything, more vengeful, until Hyde persuaded them to moderate their demands. In its final form, the bill of indemnity excluded thirty men from pardon as to life or estate, but declared a general indemnity for all offences since 1637 and laid down penalties for maliciously raking up the past.

For Charles, the indemnity was politically essential. Until it passed, the army would not disband and the City would lend no money: there were many former Parliamentarians among the aldermen and rich merchants. It was also necessary to start to heal the divisions left by civil war, so that normal life could resume. He showed some impatience at the Houses' ghoulish bickering and, outwardly, urged 'mercy and indulgence'. Only occasionally was there a hint of the bitterness he must have felt, notably in his hounding of Sir Henry Vane (not a regicide) who was executed in 1662. In general, however, Charles suppressed his desire for revenge and gave his assent to the indemnity bill on 29 August.

A second problem created by the civil wars was that of land sales. These were of three basic types. First, after the abolition of bishops in 1646 their lands were sold off, followed by those of deans and chapters.* Second, the lands confiscated from Royalist and Catholic 'delinquents' were first leased out and later sold. Third, most of the Crown's estates were sold off after the abolition of monarchy. The total income from these sales exceeded six million pounds, so many people had cause to fear financial loss when the king returned, including some whom the king wished not to upset, notably members of the army, the Presbyterian politicians who helped organise his return and City merchants, whose loans kept government going in these early months. The Declaration of Breda had referred the matter to Parliament. Monk proposed that most purchases of Crown and Church lands should be confirmed, with the purchasers paying a part of their annual value to the original owners, while Royalists should be able to regain their estates if they refunded the purchase price, plus interest [*Doc. 7*].

The former proposal was made the basis of two bills, neither of which passed. Although the king had referred the matter to Parliament, perhaps to avoid any firm commitment to the purchasers, it could not agree on what to do: the matter was too complex to be settled by general legislation, because individual circumstances varied so widely. Often tenants had bought land which they had formerly leased, or land was bought to be held in trust for its original owners. Sometimes Church lands and impropriated tithes had been used to augment the income of a parish minister. Given such variation, many cases could be settled fairly only if considered on their particular merits.

The Convention's inability to resolve the matter left the initiative to others. The Surveyor-General began to resume possession of Crown lands in July, following an order from the Lords (never ratified by the Commons). Bishops and other ecclesiastics granted new leases as if they had never been deprived of their estates. In each case, compensation was negotiated individually with the purchasers, who often continued to lease the land which they had purchased. These improvised procedures were given greater consistency in October, when the king set up a commission of sales, to decide the compensation to be paid to purchasers of Crown and Church lands. Royalists and Catholics had to seek redress in the courts, but if their estates had been confiscated they were often successful. Only those who had sold land in order to pay fines had no hope of compensation.

For such a potentially contentious issue, the land question was settled remarkably amicably. One reason was that purchasers were allowed reasonable compensation, especially if they were politically influential, while some of the largest purchasers could not demand compensation, having forfeited their estates under the Act of Indemnity. Many purchasers, perhaps the majority, had recouped their investment before 1660, the lands having been sold comparatively cheaply. Where tenants had purchased land they formerly leased, it made little difference to them to revert to leasing, especially if the rent was moderate. Many Royalists and Catholics had regained their lands before 1660, through intermediaries. For these reasons the land settlement left little lasting rancour, except among the minority of Royalists who had lost heavily or recovered their lands at the price of a crushing burden of debt. Certainly, few influential purchasers had cause to complain [63; 64; 125].

The third immediate problem was to pay off the army and part of the navy; both contained many religious and political radicals and were expensive to maintain. Charles had promised at Breda to pay the officers and soldiers their arrears and to take them into his service on the same terms. The matter was, however, outside his control. He had no direct authority over the army, as Monk was commander-in-chief and the Convention took responsibility for paying the forces. All Charles could do was to raise the militia,* supplemented by gentlemen volunteers, to guard against any attempt by the army to re-establish a republic. That apart, he had to wait until Monk and the Convention saw fit to act. Monk took his time.

Weeding out 'disaffected' officers was a slow business and he could demand favours, for himself and others, only so long as he remained the only man who could control the army.

By early July Charles had abandoned any thought of keeping up the army, and his spokesmen urged that it should be paid off quickly. They were supported by some Presbyterians who saw it as a threat to liberty [*Doc. 16*]. The majority of the Commons, however, would not consider the army until the indemnity had been settled. Indeed, it was most unlikely that the army would disband peacefully until that had passed. Bills were then passed to pay the soldiers' arrears and to allow them to practise trades as if they had completed an apprenticeship.

Together, these measures eased the reabsorption of soldiers into civilian life. A committee of six peers and twelve MPs was set up to pay off the army; it proceeded slowly because of insufficient funds. Anxious forecasts that the army might, as in 1647, refuse to disband proved mistaken. This owed much to Monk's careful purges of the officer corps and to the care taken to satisfy the army's professional expectations. Changes in the upper ranks over the past year or two had weakened the bonds between officers and men and many soldiers were pressed men or fought purely for pay; the political activism of the rank and file, so apparent in 1647–9, had diminished thereafter. The army had first become involved in politics because Parliament insensitively refused to settle its professional grievances: no such mistake was made in 1660. A few irreconcilable republicans plotted or went into exile, but most of the once formidable New Model disappeared quietly into civilian life.

Thus by the end of 1660 three of the thorniest problems created by the recent upheavals were well on the way to being resolved. On others, such as the constitution and religion, agreement was to prove more difficult.

The extent of the king's authority was, in 1660, open to argument. His power to raise revenue without Parliament's consent had been drastically curtailed in 1641 by legislation to which Charles I had assented. He had also agreed to Acts taking away Star Chamber* and High Commission* and requiring Parliament to meet at least once every three years. Later he had been stripped of other powers without his consent, starting with his control of the militia. After he left London early in 1642, the Long Parliament took over his executive functions, including the making of policy, the administration of justice and the raising and spending of money. Once the king had been defeated, a majority in Parliament was ready to lay down many of these responsibilities, provided he agreed to certain restrictions on his authority. Most MPs had no desire to direct the nation's government, but they were also determined to ensure that Charles should never again abuse his powers as he had in the 1630s. They therefore demanded what they saw as sufficient security against royal misrule: that Parliament should share with the king control over the armed forces and the selection of ministers and councillors, so that he would be unable to use force against his people or to appoint ministers who might advise him to do so. He would concede neither, and deadlock ensued, until the abolition of monarchy made the question of the extent of the king's powers irrelevant.

The Convention had to consider how much of the legislation of the 1640s should stand and whether Charles should be pressed to agree to restrictions which his father had refused to concede. Before he returned, both Houses set up committees to consider the legislation passed since 1641, in order to decide which ordinances should be repealed: this implied that others should stand. Neither committee reported, but several bills were introduced which would substantially have restricted the king's power, by depriving him of his control over the executive and the militia and his power to appoint officers of state and even members of his own household. It was also proposed that a series of bills should implement the promises in the Declaration of Breda [*Docs. 7, 11, 12*]. The bills failed because of Royalist obstruction and a simple lack of time. The declaration said nothing about the king's powers: he clearly wished to enjoy all those of his predecessors. Once he had returned without preconditions the bargaining position of those who wished to restrict his authority was weakened. They pinned their hopes on a bill to confirm the privileges of Parliament and the fundamental laws. After a leisurely progress through the Commons, who were preoccupied with the indemnity, this bill went up to the Lords on 3 July, where it stuck in committee,* despite reminders from the Commons.

The bill [*Doc. 13*] set out a list of 'fundamental laws' to be confirmed. These included Magna Carta and the legislation of 1641 against Star Chamber, High Commission and Charles I's fiscal devices; there was no explicit mention of the Triennial Act.* There were two reasons why Charles should have disliked this bill. First, as later became clear, he wished to have some of the legislation of 1641 repealed. Second, the bill would confirm not only those statutes specified but all others for the defence of the privileges of

Parliament and the liberties of the subject 'against arbitrary and illegal proceedings and taxes'. This could be construed to include some or all of the legislation of the Long Parliament and was probably intended to do so. There can be little doubt that the king used his influence in the Lords to block the bill. So long as it remained before the Lords' committee, the Commons saw no need to put forward other proposals, so the question of the king's authority was left unresolved. From his point of view this was not unsatisfactory: at least he reserved his position.

There was a similar lack of resolution about the royal revenues until the end of the session. Initially the Convention, following the practice of the Long Parliament, kept the raising and spending of money in its own hands. The customs and excise* were renewed for short periods and a Commons' committee investigated arrears in the latter. Direct taxes on land (assessments) were voted for a few months at a time. The revenues designated to pay off the army were kept, not in the royal Exchequer, but in the Chamber of the City of London, and were paid out by a parliamentary committee. The Convention had no intention of abandoning its control of financial administration until the disbanding of the army was well advanced.

If some MPs hoped to use that control to extort concessions from the king, they failed to carry their colleagues. From the outset, the Convention accepted that he should have some revenues of his own. As most of the Crown's traditional revenues had been abolished or circumscribed in 1641, such a revenue would have to be granted by Parliament. On 3 May – more than three weeks before the king's return – the Commons ordered that a bill be brought in to abolish feudal tenures. This would confirm the abolition of wardship* by an ordinance of 1645, but whereas the king had received no compensation either for this or for the revenues abolished in 1641, he was now to receive £100,000 a year, from a tax on land.

The precise form of this compensation was not settled for another six months, during which time the Commons moved slowly towards a permanent provision of revenue. On 19 June they voted to grant the incoming king the customs (tonnage and poundage) for life, as had been the practice over two centuries, with the single exception of Charles I in 1625. The Commons took some weeks to fix the rates on each commodity, but the Act received the royal assent on 28 July. It marked the first major step towards re-establishing the principle that the king should 'live of his own': that he should have a revenue for life, to support the cost of day-to-day government. Traditionally the king's 'own' had consisted in large part of 'domanial' revenues – those stemming from the Crown's hereditary landed estates (demesne) and feudal authority, which he enjoyed independently of Parliament. By 1660 the Crown's landed estates had been much reduced by sales and the ravages of war and they were to provide only a tiny fraction of Charles II's income; its feudal rights, as we have just seen, were abolished. In their place, the Crown's regular or ordinary revenue was now to come from taxes, granted by Parliament, for life or in perpetuity. England had moved from being a 'demesne state' to a 'tax state' [39; 40; 42].

Earlier, Finch and the 'court' element had blocked a proposal to set up a committee to regulate the excise, so leaving the way open for the king to resume control of the administration of the revenue. The 'court' also thwarted a move to make the grant of the customs conditional on the passage of the indemnity bill, the House stressing 'the entire confidence they have in His Majesty's goodness and relying on his royal word to pass the same afterwards' [10 VIII, *p. 104*].

The 'court' did not get everything its own way. It failed to remove from the customs bill a clause that the duties specified 'and no other' were to be levied: there was to be no return to the impositions* (non-parliamentary import duties) raised by James I and Charles I.

The grant of the customs did little to solve Charles's immediate financial problems. He had returned with little ready money, an expensive court to maintain and many calls on his generosity or gratitude. This was the first revenue he received and on 29 August he claimed it had all gone towards paying off the army. Following his complaint a committee was set up to consider his revenue. Having examined figures for Charles I's revenue and expenditure, and the current cost of the much enlarged navy, the House resolved without a division that the king needed a regular annual revenue of £1,200,000 to cover the normal costs of government in peacetime. It also accepted the committee's recommendation that bills be brought in to regulate the post office, the Crown lands and the sale of wine licences, with a view to maximising the income from these sources and so minimising the amount that would have to be raised by taxation. The House resolved to ask the king not to lease out royal estates too cheaply, or on long leases, a sensitive issue when he was inundated with petitions for such favourable treatment.

Quite how the figure of £1,200,000 was arrived at is uncertain, but there is no evidence that Charles thought it unsatisfactory. At this stage he and his financial officials can have had only the haziest idea of the true cost of the government or of the extent of its indebtedness, because so much routine financial business was still being handled by parliamentary committees. The fact that Finch was elected chairman of the committee suggests that the 'court' was well represented there. Only time would show that the annual cost of government was greater than that estimated in 1660, and the problems which this created were exacerbated by the burden of debt left by the previous regime and by the initial failure of Charles's revenues to attain their expected yield [42]. As far as his revenue was concerned, Charles must have felt, when the Convention adjourned, that a satisfactory settlement was not far off.

Questions of religion proved less tractable. The 1559 Church settlement initially pleased very few. For many committed Protestants, or Puritans,* the Church was 'but halfly reformed'. They wished to purge the Prayer Book services of their remaining 'Popish' rituals and to place more emphasis on preaching and inspiration, less on observance and set forms. Having failed to persuade Elizabeth to change the official practice of the Church, many resorted to quiet nonconformity, omitting parts of the Prayer Book which they disliked.

In time the Puritans' militancy diminished. There were some parishes where the Prayer Book was used selectively, if at all, and where the minister and his lay allies tried to impose moral discipline on the less godly parishioners. Elsewhere, those dissatisfied with the preaching of their local minister 'gadded' to sermons elsewhere, or met privately to discuss the sermon, read the Bible and pray. In general, however, it seems probable that by James I's reign most people had become used to the Prayer Book. It had acquired the authority which, in a conservative society, came from habit. Its cycle of observances, like those of the Catholic Church, followed the farming year. Its emphasis on physical actions and set forms and prayers made it more accessible and comprehensible than Puritanism, with its more cerebral emphasis on the Word. While the Puritan minority continued to denounce the Prayer Book's imperfections, the 'silent majority' came to love or at least to accept it [100 Ch. 4].

If the Church reached a certain equilibrium under James I, it did not last. Puritans, and many conformists, were outraged by the conduct of Archbishop Laud. For Laud the Reformation had gone too far. It had reduced the stress on ritual and awe which he saw as essential elements of Christian worship; its emphasis on preaching had led to the downgrading of what was for him the central mystery of Christian worship, Holy Communion. It had undermined the clergy's spiritual authority over the laity. It had led to a cynical plundering of the Church's wealth and an unacceptable level of lay interference in its affairs.

For Laud, it was vital for the clergy to reassert themselves, to insist that God should be worshipped, with due solemnity and reverence, in every parish church. In pursuing this goal, Laud had to contend both with Puritans, who regarded ceremonies as Popish, and with the boorish rusticity of many laypeople, who saw nothing wrong with baptising babies in a bucket or dispensing Communion wine in an ale tankard. Over the years, most parish clergymen had learned to accept that neither their churches nor their parishioners could be brought to perfection. Church buildings were all too often dilapidated and dirty. Many villagers had little understanding of religion (not surprisingly, given their lack of education) and allowed their dogs and children to wander at will during services. Laud refused to compromise with human imperfection and sought to impose his own standards on the whole Church, restructuring church interiors (at the parish's expense) to make the altar, duly railed off, the focus of the service. In so doing he angered many who had had no quarrel with the Church's government and worship and opened the way for a radical Puritan minority to press for the thorough reformation which they had always demanded. Only drastic changes, they claimed, starting with the abolition of bishops, could cleanse the Church of Laudianism and Popery. In bringing down Laud they hoped also to bring down the existing Church of England.

In 1640–2 most of those who loved the Prayer Book but resented Laudian innovation were confused and demoralised: they wanted to return to the way things had been under Elizabeth and James I, but did not know how. The radicals seized their chance. For generations most educated Protestants had analysed the prophecies of Daniel and Revelation, with their dramatic and yet cryptic accounts of the apocalyptic struggles that would end with the downfall of Antichrist and the Day of Judgement, and sought to apply them to their own era. The religious wars of the 1620s and 1630s seemed to fit naturally into such a schema, but where did Charles I fit in? Neither he nor his father had taken up their 'natural' role as leaders of European Protestantism. On the contrary, Charles seemed all too friendly towards Catholics, while he and Laud were determined to bring changes into the Church which many saw as 'popish'. Last but not least, he appeared to be trying to establish absolutism, which many Protestants saw as inextricably linked with Popery: both depended on untrammelled (and brutal) authority and the utter subjugation of the people.

The events of 1640–2, with the arrival of deliverance from newly presbyterianised Scotland, the downfall of Laud and his bishops and the continued perceived threat from Popery, fitted well into this apocalyptic framework. Exhortations to godly reform abounded. Little groups of self-styled saints began to meet to seek God in a purer and holier way, untainted by the sinful majority, in anticipation of the much more dramatic separation of the sheep from the goats at the Day of Judgement. The tendency towards separatism had long been apparent but had been held in check. Now the Church's authority collapsed, opening the way to debate and experiment.

The 1640s was a decade of extraordinary religious ferment and fluidity. By 1660 the 'gathered churches' had hardened into sects, each with its own doctrines, organisation and sense of identity: most notably Independents (or Congregationalists), Baptists and Quakers. All agreed that they should be free to worship in their own way and rejected, in a way few had done before 1640, the idea of a national Church in which saints and sinners mingled indiscriminately.

The majority of thinking Protestants, however, continued to believe that a single, uniform Church was necessary for the maintenance of an ordered Christian polity, a belief confirmed by what most saw as the heretical, immoral and subversive conduct of the Ranters, Quakers and others. Any hope of simply reforming Laudian episcopacy, however, was killed by Charles's intransigence and by Parliament's need to seek Scottish military aid. The Scots Presbyterian clergy insisted that the price of that aid had to be the abolition of bishops in England.

This created serious problems for those who had no quarrel with episcopacy and who would have been content had Charles I's Church been run by men like Elizabeth's early bishops. Forced by circumstances beyond their control to abolish episcopacy, they found it difficult to establish anything else in its place. Scotland (where Presbyterianism had been re-established in 1638–40) offered an obvious model, but few laymen wanted a system which would give so much power to the clergy. Since the Reformation, laymen had come to dominate many areas of English religious life. They legislated for the Church in Parliament, appointed well over half the parish clergy and collected many ecclesiastical revenues for their own profit.

Parliament therefore created a system in which the clergy were subordinated to lay elders. It aroused little enthusiasm (and some hostility) in most parts of the country and soon lost even the support of the central government when the Presbyterians lost power in Pride's Purge. Later hopes that Oliver or Richard Cromwell might establish an effective, ordered, non-episcopal Church proved illusory. Those parish clergy who had hoped for a Puritan national Church increasingly concentrated their attention on the few truly godly people among their parishioners, effectively unchurching the rest. More constructively, some (most notably Richard Baxter) tried to counter the Quaker threat by building a loose ecclesiastical organisation from the bottom up, through county 'associations' of Presbyterian and Independent clergy [46].

Once it was clear that monarchy would be restored, most assumed that a national Church would be restored with it. Such a Church was as much a part of the old regime as the monarchy, and Charles I had, in a sense, died for the Church of England. Moreover, there was a strong attachment to Anglican practice which successive Puritan regimes were unable to break: attempts to prohibit the celebration of Christmas, for example, proved an abject failure, and the Prayer Book (though banned) continued to be widely used [100 Ch. 4].

If the Church was to be restored, two questions had to be answered. First, what sort of Church? Should it be Anglican, based on the 1559 Prayer Book and as such acceptable to a broad spectrum of conformists, or a more 'Puritan' Church, with concessions to the Presbyterians? Second, should the sects which had emerged since 1640 be allowed to worship freely or should the machinery of the law be used to force them to conform to the established Church? Thus the Church settlement hinged on the related, but separate, questions of comprehension and indulgence.

The fact that the Anglican Church was eventually restored, without concessions to the Presbyterians or toleration for Dissenters, should not lead us to assume either that it was obvious from the start that this would happen, or that Charles and Hyde wished it to happen [38]. Such a view relies too much on the hindsight of men like Baxter, as they tried to explain the dashing of their high hopes of 1660 [1]. It also takes on trust Hyde's later claim that he unswervingly promoted the Church's interests, a claim coloured by his later role as champion of intransigent Anglicanism [8]. The reality was more complex and obscure.

Charles's own religious views were masked by his ability to hide his feelings. He had a lively, if idiosyncratic, interest in theology, but had little time for formal worship and little sense of the sacred, if any. He clearly inclined to Catholicism and became a Catholic on his deathbed, but that did not stop him conforming to the Church of England until his last hours, or ruthlessly sacrificing the lives and property of innocent Catholics when politically necessary. His grandfather, Henry IV of France, had reconverted to Catholicism in order to secure his crown; Charles conformed to the established Church in order to retain his.

In 1660, the form of that Church had not yet been decided. Charles's first impression must have been that Presbyterianism was very strong, an impression which Monk and the Presbyterian councillors were eager to reinforce. By contrast, the Church of England was institutionally decayed, few of the bishops were still alive and there was little sign yet of the strength of Anglican sentiment. Prudence, therefore, suggested that the Presbyterians should be accommodated within the restored national Church. Charles had no love for Presbyterianism: he had not forgotten how the Scots clergy had forced him to denounce the sins of his parents in 1650 as the price of military aid. As with the indemnity, however, the need for reconciliation and for a broad basis of support overcame his repugnance at making concessions to his family's former enemies. Throughout 1660 he promoted, with what sincerity it is impossible to tell, changes to the Church's worship that would be acceptable to the Presbyterians. Moreover, even after the strength of Anglican sentiment became apparent, Charles continued to believe – or to allow himself to be persuaded – that the Presbyterians were too powerful to be crushed and so needed to be appeased.

Hyde's attitude is even more problematical. He believed that an episcopal Church should be restored as part of the traditional constitutional fabric and as a means of maintaining ecclesiastical order and decency, but that was not incompatible with comprehension. The majority of Presbyterians would work within an episcopal Church, provided the bishops' power was curtailed. The pernickety Baxter approved almost without demur a scheme of 'limited episcopacy' drawn up by Archbishop Ussher of Armagh. Some of Hyde's allies among the clergy, notably Bishop Morley, were willing to make concessions to bring the Presbyterians into the Church. Nevertheless, there are indications that Hyde's emotional attachment to the Church and its rituals had been intensified by its recent tribulations. Moreover, while friendly towards some individuals, he seems to have seen Presbyterians in general as inherently anti-monarchical – he held them responsible for starting the civil war – and their clergy as rigid, domineering and insatiable: any concessions would merely whet their appetite for more. If these were indeed his views, however, he mostly kept them to himself. If the king was determined to seek comprehension, Hyde had little choice but to serve him as best he could [63; 116].

The first problem facing king and Convention was that of the parish clergy. Many of the clergy in post in 1640 were subsequently deprived of their livings as 'scandalous' (Royalist or Laudian), but many more retained their places, either because they already harboured Puritan inclinations or because they were sufficiently flexible to adapt. These had all been ordained by bishops. Of those ordained in the 1640s and 1650s, some still sought episcopal ordination, even after episcopacy was abolished, while others were ordained under the Presbyterian system. Given the lack of a uniform Church order in the 1650s, many of the parish clergy of May 1660 are not easy to categorise. A few were Independents and even Baptists or Fifth monarchists; the rest were more committed to a national Church and to the parochial system. Some were inflexibly opposed to episcopacy and the Prayer Book; many others were prepared to accept both, just as they had been prepared to adapt to the changes of the 1640s and the flexibility of the 1650s. Few, on the face of it, were likely to have been intransigent champions of Laud's vision of Anglicanism [122].

When Charles returned, the ejected clergy hoped to regain their livings, while those in possession wished to keep them. On 9 May a bill was brought in to secure the latter, but it had not passed by the time Charles returned. He found himself in an awkward position. He could not simply reject the claims of clergymen who had lost their livings because of their loyalty to his father's Church, but he was unwilling to alienate the Presbyterians.

Three days after reaching London Charles issued a proclamation that no incumbent should be removed except by due process of law or order of Parliament. His aim was to prevent ejected ministers from regaining possession by force while Parliament was still considering the matter. In September an Act of Parliament decreed that ejected ministers should be restored, provided they compensated those they supplanted, but confirmed all other ministers in possession, except for the few who had petitioned for the king's death, actively opposed the Restoration or denied the validity of infant baptism.

Royalist MPs pressed for more stringent doctrinal tests, but were defeated, perhaps because the king used his influence against them: the appointments which Charles and Hyde now made to vacant benefices, mostly of men who had held livings in the 1650s, do not suggest a commitment to rigid Anglicanism. Hyde also helped to thwart an attempt by Royalists to recover impropriated tithes confiscated in the 1640s; some had been used to augment the income of parish ministers, an achievement which many Presbyterians wished to preserve. There was inevitably some disruption in 1660: ministers were ejected or reinstated in maybe 700 of England's 9,000 or so parishes, but in many cases Charles and Hyde reconciled the various conflicting interests [63].

Settling the Church's government and liturgy was more difficult, but less urgent. While the Declaration of Breda talked only of liberty to 'tender consciences', Charles had written at the same time to the Speaker of the Commons promising to propose, in due course, 'somewhat for the propagation' of the Protestant religion [10]. Monk wrote of the need to call a synod of divines to settle religion, in conjunction with Parliament [*Doc. 7*].

For the Presbyterians, four main points were at issue. First, Church government: they would accept episcopacy only if the bishops consulted with representatives of the parish clergy, as in Ussher's scheme [37]. Second, they wished to be allowed to omit features of the Prayer-Book services which they thought unnecessary or Popish, such as kneeling for Communion, wearing a surplice or using the sign of the cross in baptism. Third, they wanted parish ministers to have more power to impose moral discipline on their flocks, most notably by excommunication (exclusion from Communion). Before 1641 the main instruments of moral discipline had been the Church courts, but these (for Puritans) had been tainted by their role in suppressing nonconformity. With their abolition, in 1641, the Church lost its coercive powers over the laity. Finally, they wished Presbyterian ordinations to be accepted as valid, while Anglicans claimed that, since only a bishop could ordain a priest, those ordained by Presbyters should be reordained. The fourth item was a product of the 1640s and 1650s, but the others repeated Puritan demands for further reform going back to Elizabeth's reign.

Some Presbyterian ministers who waited on Charles at Breda came away convinced that he favoured comprehension, but he was in no hurry. Some of his emissaries supported the idea of a national synod, but that might have been seen as a way to delay any decision until more urgent matters, like the indemnity and disbanding the army, had been settled. It is unlikely that Charles welcomed a bill brought into the Commons on 27 June 'for the maintenance of the true reformed Protestant religion' [10 VIII, *p. 76*]. In a series of often ill-tempered debates in committee, some argued that the doctrine of the established Church was defined not just by the Bible (as Puritans claimed) but also by the Thirty-nine Articles, which included a statement that the Church had power to decree ceremonies. Others claimed the bill was unnecessary, as the legislation establishing the Church had never lawfully been repealed. The House eventually accepted the proposal of 'court' spokesmen, both Anglican and Presbyterian, to ask the king to call a national synod and to adjourn the debate until 23 October [*Doc. 14*]. This left the way open for Charles to arrange a settlement which avoided the entrenched positions revealed in these debates and rested on his prerogative rather than an Act of Parliament. When Parliament adjourned, in September, Hyde announced that the king would soon publish a declaration granting indulgence to those who differed from their brethren for reasons of conscience. The same day Nicholas wrote that now Parliament had adjourned, the king could think about the Church settlement.

THE SECOND SESSION

During the recess the rough consensus at court began to break down. The Presbyterian councillors may not have liked Hyde, but worked with him because he was secure in Charles's favour and the king was eager to conciliate them. Charles saw Hyde as the architect of his restoration and as a willing workhorse, ready to deal with the administration which Charles found so tedious and with the petitions which flooded in. Hyde's solemn haughty manner and the favour he enjoyed made him enemies, but in the summer of 1660 his position seemed impregnable.

By the autumn, things were changing. On 3 September the king's brother, James, Duke of York, secretly married Hyde's daughter, who was pregnant by him. James soon had second thoughts and many at court argued that such an unequal match should not be allowed to stand: Hyde came of a modest gentry background, and some alleged that he was scheming to place his grandchildren on the throne. (Charles was as yet unmarried, so James was his heir presumptive.) Charles was furious, not with Hyde, but with his brother. Although he rejected suggestions (not least from his mother) that he should have the marriage annulled by Act of Parliament, the episode convinced Hyde's enemies that he could be toppled and made Hyde work harder at maintaining the king's favour. This was shown during the recess by his part in negotiating a Church settlement.

After informal discussions with Presbyterian ministers, Hyde drew up (by 4 September) a draft of the declaration to which he referred at the adjournment. Some expressions in it displeased the Presbyterians: those favouring ceremonies, he wrote, were 'much superior in number and quality' to those who did not. Presbyterian councillors and divines set down their objections and on 22 October a revised draft was discussed at Hyde's London home, Worcester House. Most of the discussion concerned comprehension, but Hyde also proposed 'that others also may be permitted to meet for religious worship' [1 I, part II, *p. 277*] provided they did not disturb the peace. Baxter protested that this might allow liberty to Papists and the matter was dropped [1; 33; 63]. Next day the king ordered two of the more moderate bishops to meet a small group of Presbyterian divines and councillors to try to reach agreement on reordination.

On 25 October the Worcester House Declaration was published. It avoided questions of theological right and wrong, and argued pragmatically the need for peace and order, for a single Protestant Church to guard against Popery and for the subordination of the ecclesiastical to the civil power. It avoided the vexed point of reordination, but on other matters gave the Presbyterians much of what they wanted. Bishops were to be assisted by suffragans and rural deans. The parish clergy were to have much more power to exclude errant parishioners from Communion. Revision of the Prayer Book was to be referred to a synod containing equal numbers of Anglicans and Presbyterians, but meanwhile incumbents could omit ceremonies or parts of the Prayer Book which were against their consciences [*Doc. 15*].

It has been claimed that this Declaration was a ruse to lull the Presbyterians until they could be crushed by a more Anglican Parliament [38]. This seems most implausible. The trend of Charles's religious policy in 1660 was consistently towards accommodation with the Presbyterians, for essentially political reasons. He delayed appointing new bishops and when he did (August) he offered bishoprics to three Presbyterians (Calamy, Reynolds and Baxter) and told the French ambassador he thought they would accept, although only Reynolds did. Of the other bishops he appointed, only John Cosin could really be seen as a 'Laudian' [63].

Meanwhile, a second strand of policy began to emerge. However broad the established Church might be, there would be many outside it. These included the sectaries, numerous enough to cause trouble if provoked, and the Catholics, who had served the Stuarts well and for whom Charles had considerable sympathy. These could not be brought within the Church, but they might be granted the indulgence promised at Breda. That promise (drafted by Hyde) had been restricted to those who 'do not disturb the peace of the kingdom', which to Hyde ruled out most of the sects and probably the Catholics. Thus when he proposed on 22 October that 'others' should be able to worship freely, he was probably acting on orders: Charles's waspish reply to Baxter's remarks about the Papists showed where his sympathies lay [1].

In a revealing letter of 23 October, Bishop Morley wrote that he was eager to have the Worcester House Declaration published

> which I hope will give abundant satisfaction to the honest and peaceably minded men of both parties, and make them cease to be parties any longer, but unanimously to join against the common enemy, the Papists, who will grow much more insolent than ever they were if somewhat be not quickly done to prevent it; for the queen will be in England on Monday, which will be a great countenance and encouragement to them. [17 III, *p. 111*]

The reference to the queen mother's imminent arrival helps explain Hyde's behaviour. Dr Green has argued persuasively that Hyde had little enthusiasm for the Declaration but was acting on orders. His absence (and Baxter's) from the meeting called on the 23rd is significant: both were likely to hinder agreement [63]. Well aware that his daughter's marriage had shaken his standing at court, Hyde was in no position to defy the king. Charles had every reason to feel satisfied. The Declaration was generally welcomed by Presbyterians and the Anglicans were as yet too disorganised to protest. As the settlement outlined in the Declaration rested on his authority, not Parliament's, it could be modified if need arose. Nicholas wrote that the king had taken the most contentious issue (Church government) into his own hands, so could hope for a successful session of Parliament [4].

The Commons, on reassembling, resolved to thank the king for the Declaration and voted to bring in a bill to implement its provisions. This was not to the king's liking and he managed to get it rejected by twenty-six votes on 28 November. The debates give no indication of the position of the 'court' Presbyterians, except Morrice, who was against the bill. The Anglicans were solidly against it and they were supported by the few Independents in the House. The king thus prevented a definite decision and kept his options open.

On two matters he did want a clear-cut decision. One was the militia, the only regular military force in early Stuart England, as there was no standing army. The legal status of the militia was very confused. Charles I had not agreed to the militia ordinance of 1642, which vested control in Parliament, but it had been neither repealed nor declared null and void. His son acted as if he possessed all his predecessors' powers over the militia, which presumably rested on the Statute of Winchester of 1285, Tudor militia legislation having lapsed in 1604. A week after his return he was issuing commissions to lords lieutenant and deputies in the traditional way. They were instructed to raise the militia rates prescribed by an Act passed by the restored Long Parliament in March – an Act whose legality he presumably did not accept [79]. Given the army's uncertain loyalty and the danger of popular disaffection, he needed a military force which, unlike the army, was under his own command. Besides, many ex-Royalists were eager to take up arms to guard against, or harass, those they saw as 'disaffected'. Most of the lords lieutenant were Royalist in sympathy, as were their deputies; in many counties bands of gentlemen volunteers continued as well.

Some militia officers were over-zealous, to say the least. By November stories abounded of acts of petty tyranny, including arbitrary imprisonment of the supposedly disaffected, conduct made more unpalatable by uncertainty about the legality of the officers' authority [91; 130]. In November and December the Commons debated the militia several times. Some MPs believed it should be regulated in order to protect the subject, but when a bill was put before the Commons, they denounced its provisions, claiming that it would establish martial law and even a regime like that of Cromwell's Major-Generals. Many were not 'forward to confirm such perpetual and exorbitant powers by a law' [21 II, *p.* 7] – even Finch had reservations – and the bill did not pass.

The other outstanding issue was the revenue. The Presbyterians tried to delay matters, hoping to force the king to allow the Worcester House bill to pass. Slowly the 'court' wore them down. The bill abolishing feudal tenures passed at last, but the king's compensation was now to be half the excise rather than £100,000 a year on land. This change reflected not so much a wish to shift the burden from land to the consumer as an inability to agree how to apportion the load and a feeling that, with a six months' assessment voted to pay off the army, land was already paying more than its fair share. Whatever the reason for the change, calculations that half the excise would be worth more than £100,000 a year proved to be correct [42].

Later, after voting by a majority of two not to grant the king the other half of the excise, the House changed its mind, despite pleas that the yield of the king's revenues should be investigated first. Charles believed that the excise would take his annual revenue well above £1,200,000, which shows how badly informed he and his financial officials were. Despite all the Presbyterians' efforts to delay it (especially after the Worcester House bill was rejected) the excise bill had also passed all its stages when the Convention was dissolved on 29 December.

Charles had announced the coming dissolution on 20 November. His decision to bring the Convention to an end can have had nothing to do with the vote not to grant the second half of the excise, which was on the 21 November. The most likely reason was that given by the Venetian resident – the 'unquiet spirit' of the Commons, especially on religion. Charles may also have resented the vehement criticism of the lords lieutenant and of the militia bill.

Even so, he cannot have been too dissatisfied with the Convention's record. It had settled the problems of indemnity, disbanding and land sales and had gone some way towards providing an adequate revenue. It had failed to limit his prerogatives and to turn his Declaration into a bill. If it had not passed the militia bill, it had not challenged his (questionable) right to control the militia. There is little evidence that he was planning to abandon the Presbyterians. The day he announced his decision to dissolve Parliament he promoted three Presbyterian lawyers. All the signs were, wrote one of the queen mother's servants, that the monarchy would be re-established 'at the highest point that has ever been' [140]. There was every reason to expect the next Parliament to continue in similar vein.

3 THE RESTORATION SETTLEMENT: THE CAVALIER PARLIAMENT

The last weeks of 1660 saw signs of major political change. Since the king's return the major theme had been reconciliation. The even balance within the Convention prevented the adoption of extreme measures. At court Clarendon co-operated with the Presbyterians because the king insisted on conciliation. In the provinces the Royalist gentry took time to regain confidence and to establish themselves in office, while the radicals lay low and the army disbanded quietly.

By November, however, Royalist officials were harassing Parliamentarians and sectaries. Plots in December and Venner's small but alarming rising in January created great alarm, an alarm sustained by rumours of risings over the next few years. These rumours increased the vindictiveness of local Royalists and they tried to crush completely the remnants of the 'good old cause'.

This Cavalier backlash found expression in the parliamentary elections early in 1661. The Royalism of the majority of MPs made probable much more partisan measures. The king could no longer play one faction off against the other, but this would create few problems provided MPs approved of his conduct of government. It soon became apparent, however, that if they did not they would have no qualms about defying him and seeking to impose their will upon him.

The polarisation in the provinces, with the counterpoint of Cavalier repression and radical plotting, evoked an ambivalent response from the government. On one hand, Charles still tried to conciliate the Presbyterians. On the other, he tried to extend his authority and powers of coercion, both as an end in itself and as a means of coping with sedition.

The tension between conciliation and repression was heightened by growing factional divisions at court. The ascendancy of Hyde, created Earl of Clarendon in April 1661, was first shaken by the scandal surrounding his daughter's marriage. The council was still divided between Anglicans and Presbyterians, but with the election of the new Parliament the latter's usefulness to the king decreased: no longer could they play a vital part in managing the Commons. While their influence subsisted, they gave support to Clarendon in his opposition to violent methods and his preference for caution and legality. 'The men are impatient to have all done at once,' he remarked on one occasion, 'but it must be done by degrees' [4 1660–1, *p. 264*].

Clarendon's caution left him open to accusations of lack of zeal for the king's service. His most outspoken critic was the Earl of Bristol. Debarred from office by his Catholicism, he was active in court intrigue, alleging that Clarendon had deliberately neglected opportunities to maximise the royal revenue and to establish a standing army [*Doc. 17*]. Clarendon certainly believed very firmly in the ancient constitution and the rule of law, but the conduct of the Convention and Cavalier Parliament suggests that neither was nearly as willing to enhance royal power as his critics claimed.

Apart from Bristol, Clarendon's leading critic was Sir Henry Bennet. Like Bristol he had been no friend of Hyde's in exile and on returning to England in April 1661 he used his courtly charm to insinuate himself into Charles's favour. The criticisms which he and Bristol made were echoed by those courtiers whom Clarendon called 'the little people', who amused the king by mocking the pompous chancellor. They found patrons in the king's mistress, Lady Castlemaine, and, after her return in 1662, the queen mother, who became the focus of an increasingly powerful Catholic interest. Their first major success came in October 1662 when Bennet superseded Nicholas as Secretary of State.

Throughout, Bennet and Bristol exploited Charles's irritation with the lectures Clarendon gave him. Their talk of strengthening the monarchy appealed to an essentially insecure king and they were ready – in Bristol's case, eager – to try to improve the position of Catholics. It would probably be misleading to see concern for Catholicism as the key to Charles's policies – he did not feel that strongly about any religion and always put self-preservation first – but he felt Catholics had long been harshly treated, so favoured the repeal of the more draconian laws against them.

This put Clarendon in an awkward position. Less rabidly anti-Catholic than most of his contemporaries, he thought it unwise to favour them too openly. Moreover, if the laws against Catholics holding office were removed, Bristol and other court Catholics would gain in influence. As the king ordered him not to oppose moves to help the Catholics, Clarendon had to obey, but his compliance did him little good as he was accused of stirring up trouble underhand [63; 97].

Such assaults on his position distressed him. He wrote to Ormond in September 1662

The worst is, the king is as discomposed as ever and looks as little after his business, which breaks my heart and makes me and other of your friends weary of our lives. He seeks for his satisfaction and delight in other company, which do not love him as well as you and I do. [17 III, *p. 222*]

Rumours that he would be dismissed proved premature. Charles was too astute to deprive himself of a loyal, hardworking servant (even if he was often prostrated by gout) or to place all his reliance on one faction, however amusing it might be. Bristol fell from favour after attempting to impeach Clarendon in 1663, but Bennet's influence continued to grow.

The factionalism at court, the unwise policies of Bennet and Bristol and their inept attempts at parliamentary management together soured the relationship of king and Commons. MPs expected frugal and honest government, support for the Church and firm measures against political and religious dissidents. Charles satisfied none of these expectations. Most Royalists felt that Parliamentarians had received too many favours (although this seems in fact to have been true only at the highest levels of government) and there were many complaints about the court's corruption and rapacity.

This groundswell of dissatisfaction encouraged court politicians to carry their feuds into the Commons, initiating attacks on the alleged misdeeds of their rivals. In 1663 there were investigations into sales of offices (especially to Parliamentarians) and into the management of the revenue: Clarendon's friend Southampton was Lord Treasurer and they had many clients in the revenue administration. The French ambassador wrote that Charles's ministers were so eager to destroy each other that the sky could fall without their noticing. Bennet and Bristol also claimed that they could manage Parliament more efficiently than Clarendon, who relied on informal chats with his old cronies. Bennet argued the need for careful canvassing and systematic distribution of rewards, but there was a major row when it was alleged that Bristol's ally, Sir Richard Temple, had 'undertaken' to manage the Commons. In fact, such management could work only if most MPs approved of the king's conduct of government. Bennet and his friends blamed Clarendon for the essentially spontaneous opposition to the king's ecclesiastical policy. Clarendon denounced Bennet's 'weak and unskilful' management, claiming that 'if we do not commit great faults . . . that body will serve the crown to a degree none ever did' [141 *fo. 45*].

The Cavalier Parliament was as loyal as any Charles was likely to find. It was more willing than the Convention to enhance his authority, but not to the point where it could threaten the liberty and property of the Anglican gentry. MPs were willing and eager to abandon the executive role which Parliament had taken up in the 1640s and which the Convention continued, in disbanding the army. Such a role involved too much time and effort. Most MPs had no wish to be professional politicians or administrators. Few received wages and to stay in London was expensive and sometimes unhealthy. Most were country squires, whose roots lay in their shires. Merchants and lawyers had businesses and practices to run. Parliament's assumption of a major role in government had been the product of exceptional circumstances, which no longer applied. MPs wished to return to normality, which meant government by the king, his councillors and officials. Those ambitious for government office could seek it in the king's service.

Not only did the Cavalier House of Commons want the king to govern, they wanted him to govern effectively. Until 1640, the main threat to the constitutional and ecclesiastical order had seemed to come from above, from Charles I and Laud, from 'Popery and arbitrary government'. From 1640 it became clear that they could also be threatened from below, by political and religious radicals and by popular involvement in politics, which the gentry and urban elites had always regarded as their exclusive preserve. There was thus support for measures that would make the king better able to hold down these disruptive forces, but not for any which might allow him to construct the sort of quasi-absolutist regime which had seemed to be developing in the 1630s. Vengeful Royalists, in Parliament and the provinces, were all in favour of measures which allowed them to persecute their former enemies, but had little time for any which might allow the king to oppress *them*; they were especially wary of a standing army. While allowing the king to resume control of the executive and providing a revenue sufficient (on paper) to support his government, they would not give so much that he could do without Parliament. They did not want Parliament to govern; they wanted it to meet regularly to scrutinise and criticise the king's conduct of government and wished the king to be sufficiently in need of money for its criticisms to be heeded. Despite its Royalism, the Cavalier Parliament could not be taken for granted, as was clearly seen in its early years [73; 94; 116].

SECURITY AND THE MACHINERY OF COERCION

Rumours of plots and Venner's rising led to orders to call out the militia, to search the houses of suspect persons for arms, to break up conventicles* and to imprison those who stirred up sedition. These orders were often obeyed with excessive enthusiasm: a proclamation was issued against searching houses without a warrant.

Concerned for his safety, Charles raised a regiment of foot and another of horse; the cost of these, and of his life guards, was to be met by disbanding garrisons in inland towns. By March 1661 the alarm had subsided, but Charles was still nervous. When Parliament met in May, he urged the Houses to confirm the Act of Indemnity and other Acts passed by the Convention, but also to deal severely with those who still acted on republican principles.

This showed the tension between his earlier concern for conciliation and a newer emphasis on authority and repression. On one hand, he still sought a broad Church settlement and tried to restrain the more extravagant Royalists: the Earl of Derby was summoned to explain his refusal to accept non-Royalists as deputy lieutenants* in Lancashire. On the other, fear of plots led to orders to arrest and imprison suspicious persons. Late in 1662 half a dozen alleged plotters were hanged to show that they had been involved in conspiracy and only Clarendon's legal scruples prevented others being sent to Louis XIV's galleys. Above all, Charles sought to strengthen his means of coercion, the militia and the army.

The first major move against 'disaffection' owed more to the Commons than to the king and showed their differing priorities. In June 1661 a bill was brought into the Commons to regulate municipal corporations. Whereas the king appointed county magistrates and officials, most towns elected their own. In the 1640s many Royalists were ejected from municipal office. Since the king's return some had been reinstated, often at the king's request, and their Parliamentarian replacements removed, but many 'disaffected' men remained in office. The Commons proposed to appoint commissioners to remove such men and install 'well-affected' persons in their place. The Lords wished to replace this plan for a purge with one to give the king sweeping powers to appoint key officials. Boroughs were to be forced to take out new charters (presumably restricting their autonomy) and to become subject to the jurisdiction of the county JPs.

The Commons were indignant. Their bill would purge disaffected members of corporations without destroying the towns' privileges and autonomy, as the Lords' amendments would [*Doc. 18*]; they rejected them without a division. When the matter was raised again after the summer recess, the Lords accepted what was, in substance, the Commons' original bill (95; 116). It seems clear that the initiative for the bill came from the Commons and that the Lords' amendments expressed the wishes of the court.

The commissioners appointed under the Act did their job thoroughly. They had the power to remove anyone who refused to take the oaths of allegiance and supremacy, an oath against resisting the Crown and a declaration against the Covenant.* They could even remove anyone who had satisfied these conditions whom they still considered 'disaffected'. They were then to fill vacant places as they judged fit. Although some, like the Earl of Derby, thought the commissioners were not rigorous enough, they implemented changes more sweeping than any of the previous twenty years, much to the Cavaliers' satisfaction; in some Kentish boroughs the commissioners disfranchised many freemen, even though they were not members of the corporation. Both king and Commons must have been well pleased that the purges were carried through without serious disturbance.

For Charles, removing the 'disaffected' from corporations was less important than strengthening his military resources. In the spring of 1661 he had only three regiments of guards and his control of the militia lacked a statutory basis. He clearly expected Parliament to make the militia more serviceable. In July it passed a bill stating that the king alone should direct the militia, but it took longer to lay down its precise form. In December the Commons heard of a plot to seize deputy lieutenants in Lancashire and a committee was set up to consider how to make the militia more effective.

Clarendon then proposed a committee of both Houses to investigate the alleged plot over the Christmas recess and to consider proposals for a professional force, at least on a temporary basis, so that the militia need not be constantly on duty. Many saw in this a design to establish a standing army. Taken aback by this reaction, Clarendon referred the whole matter back to Parliament. After much debate, the Commons resolved to raise a temporary auxiliary force of 1,200, out of the militia, but even this project for a more professional 'select militia' was later dropped.

Instead, the Commons resolved that the militia should continue as it was, but that the king should have the power to raise up to £70,000 a year for three years, through the militia rate. This would enable the militia to respond swiftly to emergencies. Some problems remained: for example, the Commons disliked a proposal that the militia should be able to enter property forcibly in daytime. The bill finally passed in May 1662 [116; 130].

The summer of 1662 was an anxious time, with the new militia not yet settled and fears of disorder when the Church settlement came into force in August. Five more army regiments were ordered to be raised in September and in December the lords lieutenant were ordered to levy the £70,000 for that year. In 1663 an Act allowed each militia unit to be kept on foot for up to fourteen days, which meant that part could always be on duty, except during the harvest and the depths of winter. By late 1663 Charles could feel more confident of his ability to deal with disturbances. The new militia was settled under politically reliable officers, with funds provided until the end of 1664. His army – regular regiments and independent companies in garrisons – now amounted to more than 8,000 men. Parliament resisted anything which might imply recognition of a 'standing army' (identified with tyranny), but raised no real objection to the king's keeping up these forces at his own expense as 'guards and garrisons'. Widely dispersed, they did not seem to threaten Parliament or people and their relations with the civilian population were often good. A rough balance had been achieved between the security of the state and the liberty of the subject. Charles did not think his military resources were adequate, but he was still the first English king to have even a small standing army in peacetime [44; 49].

THE CONSTITUTION AND THE KING'S REVENUE

The Convention had done little to define the king's powers. The bill to confirm the fundamental laws did not pass and did not say how much of the legislation of 1640–60 remained in force. By contrast, the Act for the Safety and Preservation of His Majesty's Person and Government, the first passed by the new Parliament, declared null and void all acts which had not received the royal assent. Thus the fiscal legislation of 1641, the Triennial Act and the Acts taking away Star Chamber and High Commission were to stand, as was that excluding the bishops from the Lords, but the militia ordinance and all subsequent legislation were nullified.

This did not mean that the legislation to which Charles I had assented should be preserved inviolate, as the Convention's bill had proposed. The Act excluding the bishops from the Lords was soon repealed, as was that part of the Act against High Commission which abolished other Church courts. In 1662 and 1663 the Lords considered repealing all the legislation of the Long Parliament, re-enacting only such bills as they thought fit. A committee considered how to set up a court as useful to poor litigants as Star Chamber, while guarding against the abuses of the 1630s. In 1664, at the second attempt, Charles secured the passage of a new Triennial Act which expressed the hope that the king would call Parliament often – at least every three years – but, unlike that of 1641, established no machinery to make him do so and laid down no minimum length for sessions.

If the Cavalier Parliament considered repealing some of the Acts of 1641, it was also reluctant to confirm those of the Convention concerning the indemnity, the confirmation of judicial proceedings and the abolition of wardship. In May the Commons considered a bill to grant an indemnity to the king's faithful subjects and to restore estates wrongfully taken from them, which would overturn both the Indemnity Act and many legal judgments of 1642–60. Only when the king told them that his honour was engaged did the Commons comply.

In other ways, the Houses enhanced the king's authority. The Act for the preservation of his person declared the Covenant unlawful and denied that the Houses could legislate without the king. It provided for the punishment of anyone accusing the king of trying to bring in Popery or inciting the people to hate the king. Another Act was designed to prevent mass petitioning, which had often, in the 1640s, been a pretext for intimidation. Now petitions with more than twenty signatories had to be authorised by at least three JPs or a county grand jury and could be presented by no more than ten persons. Finally, the 1662 Licensing Act gave a statutory basis to press censorship for the first time: hitherto it had rested on the royal prerogative. Those writing, printing or selling unlicensed works were to be punished and it was proposed that the number of presses in London should be reduced.

The thinking behind these and the new Militia Acts was obvious: the king needed additional powers to repress the subversive forces which had emerged since 1640, which had mobilised opinion using petitions and the press and had often accused Charles I and his followers of being favourers of Popery. However, as with the militia and the corporations, the Commons showed that they were not prepared to trust the king too far. The Licensing Act was to operate for only a short period; it was renewed several times and in 1665 was extended until the end of the next Parliament: no one could have guessed that that would come in 1679. On other matters, too, king and Commons did not see eye to eye. The fiscal legislation of 1641 remained intact: MPs had no intention of allowing Charles II to raise money in ways not approved by Parliament, as his father had done. In June 1661 they resolved to impeach one John Walter for demanding dues from ships on the pretext of a ballast patent, whereupon the patent was speedily withdrawn. They reacted similarly to later patents to set up lighthouses.

On the other hand, they declared themselves willing to 'settle a full, constant and standing revenue ... such as might befit the support of so great and good a prince and might honourably and effectually maintain and uphold his government' [10 VIII, *p. 262*] and to grant a 'plentiful' supply to meet his immediate needs. Their actions proved less generous than their words. The 'immediate supply' consisted of inviting voluntary contributions, which produced £229,000 – not enough either to meet the king's expenses or to pay off his debts. As for the permanent revenue, the Secretary to the Treasury, Sir Philip Warwick, showed that the king's basic revenues were yielding some £265,000 a year less than the estimated £1,200,000. The Commons accepted this figure, and started a lengthy investigation into the administration of the excise, to see if its yield could be improved.

The Commons' slowness owed much to a lack of fiscal expertise (and perhaps numeracy). MPs always blamed shortfalls on corruption and inefficiency and were eager to accept over-optimistic estimates of what revenues would yield. Ultimately, they had no wish to grant more in taxes than they had to: they had to answer to their constituents and neighbours and had expected the disbanding of the New Model to bring a large cut in taxation [*Doc. 16*]. Besides, if they granted too much, the king might feel that he did not need to heed their advice on those issues, like religion, where their views diverged from his [*Doc. 20*].

They were not wholly unco-operative. In November 1661 they resolved to raise an assessment of £1,200,000 over eighteen months 'for the king's present occasions' – more than twice as much as the largest parliamentary grant of the 1620s – and on 1 March 1662 they gave a first reading to a bill for a hearth tax:* perhaps significantly, this followed Charles's announcement that he had approved the Prayer Book, as revised by Convocation.* The long investigation into the excise led to an Act of 1663 which in some ways strengthened the hand of the collectors, but also sought to prevent some of their misdeeds. Jurisdiction over the excise was vested in the JPs, thus giving members of the gentry power to prevent extortion and oppression [40; 42].

The spring of 1663 saw the most sustained campaign of the reign to subject the king's revenue to parliamentary scrutiny and control. This was part of the campaign to oust Clarendon and his followers. His enemies claimed that he was behind the opposition to the king's religious policy and that that opposition would disappear if the king gave the Commons satisfaction on other matters. Factious courtiers promoted investigations into 'mismanagement' in the hope of finding evidence to support their call for the removal of Clarendon and others (many of them Parliamentarians) admitted into office in 1660. A bill was brought in to ensure that offices went only to loyal subjects, who conformed to the Church of England. On the production of detailed accounts of the king's finances, various committees and sub-committees were set up to look into various branches of the revenue. Following a report suggesting that the yield could be higher, it was resolved on 8 May to bring in a bill 'for fixing the public charges of the kingdom upon some particular branches of his Majesty's revenue' [10 VIII, *p. 478*]. The king was asked to make no arrangements for managing the post office until the Commons had investigated the matter and to revoke all leases of Crown lands made for too long a time or at too low a rent. It was claimed that the revenue could be increased by £56,000, but some of the figures were decidedly hypothetical. When the Commons at last agreed to vote an immediate supply they voted a subsidy, which was antiquated and inefficient and brought in less than the free gift of 1661 [10; 40; 42].

All this might suggest that the once loyal Cavalier House of Commons was now out of control, but that was not so. These investigations reflected a mixture of endemic backbench suspicion of the misuse of power and deliberate mischief-making by court politicians. Confusion reigned: 'I can neither tell you what the House intends or what we at Whitehall wish they would,' wrote Henry Coventry [*Doc. 19*].

In fact, all the sound and fury had little lasting effect. The bill to appropriate each branch of the revenue to particular items of expenditure, which would have imposed rigid constraints on the king's finances, did not pass. The attempts to scrutinise the administration of the Crown lands and post office came to nothing. On the positive side, Acts were passed which helped to improve the administration of the excise and hearth money and the Commons cannot have foreseen the poor yield of the subsidy. The discrediting of Temple and Bristol temporarily cooled the fires of faction at court which had helped to inflame the Commons. Despite the haggling and niggling, between 1661 and 1663 the Commons had tried to fulfil their promise of a 'full constant and standing revenue', granting the hearth tax (in perpetuity) and trying to increase the yield of the customs and excise. If the increase was less than expected, this was due partly to trade depression and partly to ignorance of the problems involved: it took twenty years' trial and error to produce the much more efficient revenue system of the 1680s.

It was to be a decade before the ordinary revenue reached the magic figure of £1,200,000: thanks partly to Charles's extravagance and partly to the accumulated burden of debt, this still proved insufficient for his needs [42]. Parliament had, however, agreed that the king should once more 'live of his own' and had granted him a series of revenues to exploit as best he could, rather than a fixed annual sum. At first, this meant that he received much less than the sum which Parliament had judged necessary, but by the end of the reign, thanks to booming overseas trade and much improved management, he was receiving substantially more. As with the militia, Charles was granted less in revenue than he would have liked, but the end result was far from unsatisfactory.

RELIGION

The Cavalier House of Commons soon made its religious outlook clear by ordering MPs to take Communion according to the Anglican rite and resolving to burn the Covenant. The Act for the preservation of the king's person annulled almost all the ecclesiastical legislation of the 1640s: in the end, only the abolition of High Commission was to stand. With the decision to restore the bishops to the Lords, it was clear that the Commons wished to restore episcopacy in its old form, without the concessions to the Presbyterians set out in the Worcester House Declaration.

In fact, since his first episcopal appointments in August 1660, Charles had gradually been restoring the old established Church: the only question was whether it was going to be modified at all, to accommodate the Presbyterians. The mood of the new House of Commons made this less and less likely and in 1661–2 Charles was forced into an increasingly desperate programme of damage limitation, to try and salvage some small vestige of comprehension. By the time the new Parliament met, he accepted that a new uniformity bill was needed. Clarendon told the Houses that a 'yoke' was required, to restore order after so many years of licence. Rules were needed and rules had to be obeyed, but the rules in force in the past might be modified a little to make it easier for some weaker brethren to conform [116].

On 25 June 1661 the Commons read a bill 'to supply any defect in the former laws and to provide for an effectual conformity to the liturgy of the Church' [10 VIII, *p. 279*]. They saw no need to draft a new Prayer Book, because the legislation requiring the use of that of 1559 was still in force. The bill aimed to ensure that only those who used the Prayer Book services should remain in benefices in the established Church. It passed the Commons only to stick in the Lords, thanks no doubt to the king's influence.

Meanwhile, his attempts to achieve a measure of latitude by other means ended in failure. As promised at Worcester House, he called a synod of divines at the Savoy, but to no avail. The Presbyterians were divided and somewhat demoralised while the bishops, encouraged by the Commons' behaviour, refused to compromise. Convocation also met, as was usual in time of Parliament. The summons to its members did not include the usual provision that nothing was to be agreed contrary to the Church's liturgy or doctrine, but then Charles delayed its meeting, wary of the new mood of Anglican militancy and warned it against discussing sensitive topics [33].

Meanwhile, there was a concerted attempt to secure toleration for Catholics. The Lords resolved to bring in a bill to repeal some of the more severe laws against them, with provisions for priests to register with the secretary of state. The bill did not pass the Lords and would certainly have failed in the Commons. Charles strongly supported it and Clarendon did not oppose it openly, but public opinion was against any sort of toleration. Alarms of 'fanatic' plots reinforced the belief of most Anglicans that all Protestant Dissenters were seditious: the Commons were unconvinced by Clarendon's attempt to distinguish between peaceable and seditious Dissenters. This hardening of attitudes made it improbable that Parliament would agree to any form of indulgence.

When Parliament reconvened in November, Charles told the Houses that religion was too hard a matter for him and referred it to them. He also asked Convocation to review the Prayer Book, in the hope that it might recommend changes to make it more acceptable to Presbyterians. (This was not inconceivable: the Commons had more than once discussed incorporating some elements from the more Protestant Prayer Book of 1552.) In the event, however, Convocation recommended few changes.

While this revision was under way, the Lords held up the uniformity bill, which may have provoked the Commons to pass a bill which, far from ratifying the Convention's Act confirming ministers in their livings, would have negated it. The new bill would confirm only those who used the Prayer Book and who had been ordained by a bishop. The Lords rejected the bill, thanks mainly to Clarendon, who won over seven bishops and, for once, co-operated with Bristol [*Doc. 20*]. The Commons responded by adding most of the requirements of the ministers' bill to the uniformity bill, making it more rigorous than before. It now required ministers to declare their assent to everything in the Prayer Book and to renounce the Covenant, which many had solemnly sworn to uphold in the 1640s. Again the king, through Clarendon, tried to add an element of flexibility. On 17 March Clarendon proposed to the Lords that the king should be able to dispense any beneficed minister from wearing the surplice or using the sign of the cross in baptism [*Doc. 21*]. These were small concessions to Presbyterian incumbents compared with those in the Worcester House Declaration. Instead of a wide comprehension Charles offered only a little latitude to selected individuals, but although the Lords accepted the proposal, the Commons rejected it without a division. They also rejected a proposal that those ejected for nonconformity should receive one-fifth of the income of their parishes, a concession granted to ejected Anglicans in the 1640s, and insisted that the provisions for uniformity should be extended to non-beneficed lecturers and schoolmasters. Faced with the Commons intractability, the Lords backed down.

Charles assented to the uniformity bill, but still hoped to mitigate its rigour. Clarendon told the Houses that

the execution of these sharp laws depends upon the wisdom of the most discerning, generous and merciful prince, who having had more experience of the nature and humour of mankind than any prince living can best distinguish between tenderness of conscience and pride of conscience. [18 XI, *p. 476*]

Under the terms of the Act, ministers had to declare their conformity or quit their benefices by 24 August 1662. As the deadline approached, rumours of revolt abounded and the king's forces were on continual alert. Late in August Clarendon sent word to some London Presbyterian ministers that the king wished them to petition to be dispensed from strict compliance with the Act, with a strong hint that the petition would be granted. They petitioned, but the privy council rejected their plea after a vigorous speech from the Bishop of London. Again, Clarendon seemed to advocate conciliation, but this time he clearly acted against his own inclinations. He wrote to Ormond

> The very severe execution of the Act of Uniformity which is resolved on may, I fear, add more fuel to the matter that was before combustible enough. But we are in and must proceed with steadiness and so must you [in Ireland] and I wish I were as confident that we shall do so as that you will. [63, *p. 216*]

Whether or not he had earlier preferred conciliation – and it seems probable that (privately at least) he had not – Clarendon was now convinced that the government had no option but to enforce the Act. He seems also to have doubted whether the Presbyterians would revolt. If so, he was right. Although a total of some 1,800 ministers lost their livings, the exodus was peaceful [63].

The ambivalence of Clarendon's position was seen again in Charles's last attempt to weaken the Act of Uniformity. Late in December he issued a declaration stating his dislike of persecution and his hope that Parliament would pass legislation acknowledging his power to dispense with the Act's provisions and to reduce the burdens on Catholics [16]. This was merely a declaration of intent, which in itself did nothing for Dissenters or Catholics. Mention of the latter reflected the increased activity of the court Catholics, led by Bristol and the queen mother. The hopes expressed in the declaration that Parliament might reverse its stand on religion may seem naive. They can perhaps be explained by Charles's telling the French ambassador that he had 'taken measures' with some peers and MPs and expected them to prove amenable – probably a reference to Bennet and Bristol's new approach to parliamentary management.

Clarendon was in an awkward position. He must have regarded the declaration (especially the references to Catholics) as foolish and provocative, but if he opposed it openly he would lose the king's favour. Bennet had recently replaced Nicholas as secretary, leaving Clarendon feeling more isolated than ever. His gout offered a way out. When Bennet read him a draft of the declaration he raised various objections. When these were met, he said that declarations were a ticklish commodity and the important thing was that it should do no harm. He implied that he was in such pain that he could not concentrate but he was well enough to receive the French ambassador at about this time. When Parliament reconvened in February 1663 he claimed to be too ill to attend.

On 23 February a bill was brought into the Lords to allow the king to dispense individuals from complying with the Act of Uniformity and other laws imposing conformity or oaths in religious matters. It would also empower him to issue licences to peaceable Protestants to worship in their own way. None of these benefits was to apply to Catholics, nor could those holding benefices in the Church of England be dispensed from conforming to its liturgy. Charles was now seeking an element of toleration as well as comprehension and, although this was to be authorised by Parliament, the granting of this liberty was to be entirely at his discretion.

The Lords amended the bill to apply only to the Act of Uniformity, thus making sure that it could benefit neither Catholics nor sectaries. The Commons meanwhile resolved to draw up reasons against indulgence to Dissenters and to bring in a bill against the growth of Popery. When Clarendon reappeared in the Lords on 12 March, he moved to adjourn debate on the dispensing bill for a month, which, in effect, shelved it indefinitely.

In abandoning his attempt to give a statutory basis to his dispensing power, Charles finally accepted the Act of Uniformity. If he wished to help Catholics and Protestant Dissenters, he would have to do so by not enforcing the laws against them. His attitude to Dissenters was ambivalent. Some, he thought, were basically peaceable, but were goaded into revolt by persecution; these deserved a measure of indulgence. Others were irreconcilable and seditious and he oscillated between a policy of repression (to hold them down) and toleration (to propitiate them). He agreed to new repressive measures after the Northern Rising of 1663 (1664 Conventicle Act) and in 1665, during the Second Dutch War, the Five Mile Act, designed to drive Dissenting ministers away from their congregations and from towns. In 1667–8, after the fall of Clarendon, he again toyed with comprehension, only to revert to repression with the 1670 Conventicle Act. In 1672 he switched to toleration again, with the Declaration of Indulgence.

Far from representing a devious and successful design by Charles and Clarendon [38], the Restoration Church settlement was a humiliating defeat for the king. Political calculation inclined him to favour comprehension; the Cavalier House of Commons insisted on re-establishing a narrowly Anglican Church. The king, it would seem, not for the only time in his reign, was out of step with public opinion. In many places Anglican worship was re-established well before the Act of Uniformity; the Presbyterians were fewer and weaker than the king was led to believe, while Anglicanism went from strength to strength after 1660, reaching a peak of militancy and fervour in the reign of Queen Anne.

This is a plausible viewpoint, but one which is not entirely convincing. It relies too much on hindsight: the clergy of the 1660s were far less self-confident – and in many cases far less aggressively 'Anglican' (or High Church) – than those of the early 1680s or of Anne's reign. While those ejected in the 1640s might indeed adhere to traditional 'Anglican' values, those who had held parishes in the 1640s and 1650s were much less likely to do so. Ejected ministers and exiles kept alive and perhaps revitalised the spirit of Anglicanism, but it took time for this spirit to suffuse a new generation of ordinands: indeed it became possible only when the Church regained possession of the universities at the Restoration [122].

If the clergy of the 1660s were perhaps less 'Anglican' than the Church settlement would suggest, the same might well be true of the gentry. The legislation against Dissenters was fitfully enforced. It may well be that JPs regarded it as a necessary weapon to be used in an emergency (rather like the laws against Papists) but not on a week-by-week basis. Even MPs clearly had reservations about it: the first Conventicle Act was only temporary and lapsed in 1668. Moreover, the Cavalier House of Commons contained only a relatively small minority who can be identified as devout adherents of the Church and several divisions on the uniformity bill were surprisingly close. This has led to the suggestion that the House was carried along by the rhetoric and zeal of this highly committed and articulate minority [116]. It is impossible to be sure that this is so, as virtually no record survives of debates; but two other possibilities suggest themselves. One is that the growing rigour of the uniformity bill was an irritated response to the repeated efforts of the king (abetted by Papists like Bristol) to undermine the bill. The other is that the bill was an exercise in spite: angry at the king's supposedly undue favour to Presbyterians and at being prevented by the

Indemnity Act from pursuing them for past misdeeds, MPs sought instead to harass them for present nonconformity. (The latter argument would however apply first and foremost to sectaries: but the main victims of the Act of Uniformity were the Presbyterian clergy.) It may also be that narrowing the Church was a preliminary to excluding non-Anglicans from office, as was suggested in 1663.

Given the lack of evidence, it is unlikely that we can ever be sure of the true motives behind the religious settlement. What can be said with confidence is that the gentry did much more than the clergy to shape it. They drafted and passed legislation and took the lead in harassing and ejecting non-Anglican ministers and persecuting Dissenting congregations. The gentry's role was symbolised by the eventual passage of a bill to restore advowsons* and impropriated tithes confiscated from laymen in the 1640s. Lay domination over the Church, briefly interrupted, was restored.

This in itself was indicative of a fundamental feature of the Restoration settlement. If the king was granted extensive powers and a nearly adequate revenue, this was not because he was in a position to demand either, but because the ruling elite, as represented in Parliament, *wanted* him to have them. Nothing would have been easier than to deny the penniless Charles II a revenue adequate for his needs, but the Convention – with, it must be remembered, a sizeable proportion of ex-Parliamentarians – did no such thing. Scared by the upheavals of 1640–60, England's rulers believed that effective monarchy was necessary to maintain order, hierarchy and subordination. However, they expected the king to use those powers in a manner compatible with their interests and prejudices. How far those expectations would be met remained to be seen.

PART TWO: THE REIGN OF CHARLES II

4 SOCIETY AND GOVERNMENT

The Restoration reinforced the social order which existed before the civil war, in which wealth was very unequally distributed and the wealthy few ruled the many. Despite the rapid growth of merchant shipping and overseas trade, notably with the colonies [54], the economy remained predominantly agricultural. Manufactures were becoming more diverse and the demand for consumer goods was becoming more discerning and sophisticated, but the basic unit of production remained the household – and very often the rural household. London's population was about half a million, but the next largest town, Norwich, had little more than 20,000 inhabitants. The great majority of England's five million or so people lived in villages or small market towns: even in 1700 less than 20 per cent of the population lived in towns with more than 2,500 inhabitants – and over half of those lived in London.

Poor transport made the carriage of bulky goods expensive and encouraged a large measure of local self-sufficiency. It also inhibited the dissemination of news. The collapse of press censorship in 1640 had triggered an explosion of political publications and debate and created a hunger for political information which could not be suppressed by the reimposition of censorship in 1662. News still spread by private correspondence even though it was common knowledge that letters were often opened at the post office and by word of mouth, especially in the newly fashionable coffee-houses. The government, for its part, now tried to influence public opinion, partly through the official *Gazette*, partly through the quasi-official (and much sought after) newsletters emanating from the offices of the secretaries of state. Quite how widely this news was disseminated must remain a matter of speculation. While London and larger provincial towns boasted a high level of literacy and of knowledge of the outside world – foreigners remarked on the boldness with which Londoners discussed politics – many small towns and villages must have been much less well informed. Even so, news of the great events of the reign, for example the Popish Plot, percolated throughout the kingdom and the lapsing of censorship in 1679 was followed by a huge surge in political publishing reminiscent of the 1640s [88; 92; 99].

Despite the extensive evidence of popular interest in politics under Charles II, much of the population must still have plodded through the working year with little awareness of events at national level. For such people, little affected by religious or political radicalism, the Restoration must have made little difference, except that they could once more celebrate Christmas and other festivals and were less likely to be maltreated by soldiers.

The bulk of the landed elite, Parliamentarians as well as Royalists, was badly shaken by the events of the late 1640s and 1650s. The traditional social order seemed to be toppling, with base-born army officers ordering around members of long-established county families. The alarm which the old elite felt helps to explain the vindictiveness shown at the Restoration – especially against Quakers, the most insubordinate of the sects – and Parliament's willingness to build up the king's power, to ensure that such upheavals would not happen again.

LOCAL GOVERNMENT

Both personal inclination and political common sense led Charles to accept that the landed elite should resume its direction of local government. Unlike Louis XIV, he had no nationwide network of professional officials in the provinces until the development of the excise and hearth tax administrations in the 1680s; the customs administration had been established earlier, but was confined to port towns. Traditionally, the Crown relied on the leading men of the counties, who possessed the economic power and local standing needed to command respect and also the leisure and, it was hoped, the education and personal qualities to discharge their responsibilities diligently. The English system of local government, centred on the JPs, involved an alliance between Crown and gentry from which both benefited. The gentry enhanced their local prestige and gained the power to regulate the affairs of the locality and punish the misdeeds of the lower orders. The Crown had local government carried on and provided rewards for men of political weight at no financial cost.

It was a system of local government that grew so naturally out of

England's social and institutional order that its revival at the Restoration must have seemed inevitable. Local defence was again entrusted to the militia, itself a microcosm of county society, with gentlemen officers commanding artisans and countrymen. With land, the main source of wealth, concentrated in a few hands, such a system seemed natural; the gentry also continued to provide the bulk of the membership of the House of Commons.

In much the same way, town government usually remained the preserve of the richest inhabitants, who could support the often considerable expense of municipal office and did not need to devote all their time to a business or profession. Even in villages, the offices of constable, churchwarden and overseer of the poor were usually held by the more substantial villagers. At every level there was a considerable measure of self-government, although the circle of those who participated was usually narrow. As the king's apparatus of government and powers of coercion were weak – his standing army was small and widely dispersed – he depended heavily on the responsibility and probity of those involved in local government.

How well local governors lived up to their responsibilities varied. Parish officials were variously accused of laxity and petty tyranny. The rulers of towns showed an increasing tendency towards oligarchy and were often accused of using their position for their own profit, misusing corporation property and dining lavishly at the town's expense. Gentlemen, too, often behaved arbitrarily or selfishly. Many early Stuart landlords pushed rents up as high as the market would bear, evicted those who could not pay and tried to establish proprietorial rights over common land. Some used their power as JPs to harass the victims of such practices or turned a blind eye to the chicanery and strong-arm tactics of fellow-landowners.

On the other hand, Tudor and early Stuart governments tried to enforce a wide range of regulations designed to protect the poor against undue exploitation, notably by trying to maintain adequate supplies of grain at moderate prices. Where such preventive measures proved insufficient, the poor laws provided that those unable to work should receive money to buy food and the able-bodied unemployed should be set to work.

The cynical might argue that such measures reflected a fear of disorder. With the population rising, too many people were chasing too little food and too little work. Prices (especially food prices) rose, unemployment and underemployment grew, real wages fell. Sheer hunger might drive people to riot, as contemporaries were well aware. Fear of disorder underlay some measures, such as the severe treatment of vagrants, but behind others there was a concern for justice and even a certain compassion, as shown by the severity against grain speculators, the provision for the old, the sick and children, and the many bequests to the poor. The self-interest of the ruling elite might find expression not in the maximisation of rents, but in seeking to stand well in the eyes of the poor. Compared with most continental aristocracies, the conduct of the Tudor and early Stuart gentry towards the poor seems generally responsible and just.

ECONOMIC AND SOCIAL POLICY

After 1660 central interference in local government declined markedly. The Elizabethan and early Stuart privy council bombarded JPs with directives, culminating in the Book of Orders of 1630–1, which prescribed rigidly and in detail which laws the JPs should enforce and how. Under Charles II the demands of the king and council were limited. They expected JPs to ensure that law and order were maintained and that the royal revenue was collected. In times of political tension, JPs were ordered to search the homes of suspicious persons or to enforce the laws against Dissenters or Catholics.

On more routine matters, however, such as social and economic regulation, highways and bridges, JPs were left to their own devices. This led to a growing diversity of administrative practice, as authorities in counties and towns reacted to new problems in different ways. In many towns, householders had long been responsible for cleansing, repairing and lighting the streets outside their homes, while highways and bridges were to be maintained by the parishes in which they stood. With urban growth and the increase in wheeled traffic, such a diffusion of responsibility allowed the roads to deteriorate, so these tasks were transferred either to *ad hoc* bodies of paving or cleansing commissioners, or to the corporation or county as a whole. The responsibilities of the individual or parish were commuted into a money rate. The speed at which this process occurred, and the forms it took, varied greatly, but the outcome was that the organs of local government became more numerous and various in the century after 1660 [55; 58; 59].

Leaving JPs to their own devices also led to changes in social and economic policy, which were reflected in parliamentary legislation. Even before 1660 central government was showing less interest in regulating the grain market, perhaps because the methods used proved ineffective, perhaps because the poor law offered another means of providing for the poor, perhaps because grain prices were levelling off and even starting to fall [104]. The population rise had virtually stopped by the 1650s, prices were stabilising and real wages beginning to rise. Dearth and poverty did not disappear: there were famine prices in some areas in 1661–2, 1678–9 and above all 1709–10. Unemployment and underemployment remained endemic: many unskilled workers found work only intermittently and at low wages. In 1696 Gregory King calculated that more than half the population 'decreased the wealth of the kingdom', or consumed more than they produced. Central government, however, now showed little interest in the preventive, or palliative, measures so often ordered earlier in the century. Some magistrates still tried to enforce the old regulations on grain marketing and against speculation, especially in years of dearth, when failure to take even cosmetic action could provoke riots.

In general, however, these regulations fell into disuse. The landed elite ceased to protect the consumer, trying instead to help the producer. Grain imports were restricted, unless prices at home rose to near-famine levels. From 1673 there were various provisions for bounties on grain exports, the aim being to siphon off England's surplus production and so prevent prices falling too far in years of relative abundance. Similarly, the Act of 1666 against importing Irish cattle was intended to keep up the price of English beasts. Together with the game laws, restricting hunting rights to substantial landowners, such legislation could be seen as evidence that the landed elite became more self-centred after 1660. This could in turn be seen as a response to the way economic conditions were turning against landowners: farm prices were levelling off, profits and rents were falling.

Was the landed elite using its political power to shore up its economic position at the expense of the poor? It should first be mentioned that it is uncertain how far corn bounties and the like affected price levels (although England was unusual in not experiencing a large fall in prices after 1650) and that real wages (admittedly a statistical abstraction) rose substantially in the century after 1650. The poor relief system now raised and paid out far more than in the first half of the century. The Act of Settlement of 1662 tried to restrict eligibility for relief in any parish to those 'settled' there: newcomers and squatters could be made to move on. It seems, however, that newcomers were often treated more harshly by parish officials (who were immediately responsible to those who paid the poor rate) than by county JPs, who were often more detached, flexible and sympathetic [118; 123].

In general, the image of ruthlessly selfish landowners, oppressing all below them, seems something of a caricature. Economic circumstances militated against such behaviour. As farming became less profitable and rents fell, efficient tenants could dictate terms to landlords. Many landlords found it wiser to write off rent arrears in bad years than to have no tenants. The increased importance of electoral politics made it advisable for a politically ambitious landlord to maintain his tenants' goodwill: he might need their votes.

When one considers wider aspects of fiscal and economic policy, the idea that the landed elite was obsessively selfish becomes even harder to sustain. True, the abolition of wardship removed an occasional and irritating burden on those who held land by feudal tenures, while the king was compensated at the expense of the consumer, through the excise. It is also true that the Commons imposed no permanent tax on land and, in temporary grants, often placed the burden on trade or consumption rather than land. However, when it was necessary to raise a large sum quickly they relied on monthly assessments, which fell mainly on land: this was seen most spectacularly in the vote in December 1664 to raise £2,500,000 for a war against the Dutch. Moreover, when voting taxes on trade they showed considerable discrimination. New customs duties were designed to boost exports and inhibit imports, especially from France. A similar concern for the promotion of trade and shipping was seen in the Navigation Acts of the early 1660s which renewed and extended that of 1651. These were intended to protect England's expanding colonial trades against Dutch and other interlopers and to ensure that English shippers carried a higher proportion of the goods brought into English ports.

Such an approach to fiscal and economic matters does not suggest that the predominantly landed Parliament was concerned exclusively with the interests of landowners; many MPs had a wider conception of their responsibilities. On the other hand, because of the wealth and power of the landed elite, Charles had to retain its trust and goodwill, in local government and in Parliament. The next chapter will, therefore, deal with national politics.

5 POLITICS AND THE CONSTITUTION

IDEOLOGICAL CONSEQUENCES OF THE CIVIL WARS

The Restoration settlement showed the concern of the ruling elite (as represented in Parliament) to re-establish what it saw as the proper balance of the constitution. The king should possess the powers needed to run the government. He should choose his own advisers and officials and be responsible for the formulation of policy, at home and abroad. He should protect his subjects against revolt and invasion, maintain law and order and dispense justice. He should defend the established Church, suppress heresy and schism and promote Christian morality. He should use his powers for the good of his subjects and try to create a secure, ordered society, permeated by Christian values and the rule of law. The subject should be protected by the law against possible abuses of royal power, especially arbitrary interference with property or personal liberty. Parliaments and juries were the cornerstones of English liberties; kings could not make laws or levy taxes without consent.

Kept within these limits, monarchy seemed the most rational, effective and beneficial form of government. Democracy, it was believed, degenerated into anarchy, aristocracy slid into oligarchy, unlimited monarchy soon became tyranny, but limited monarchy combined the best features of each without the vices, reconciling order and liberty. The king needed to be strong enough to fulfil his responsibilities to his people, but not strong enough to oppress them. The constraints on him were more moral and political than legal or constitutional, but a king with limited powers of coercion, who depended so much on the voluntary co-operation of his subjects, would be wise not to antagonise them too much or too often.

Charles I exposed the fragility of this mixed and balanced constitution. If a king was determined to stretch his powers to the limit, neither the law courts nor Parliament could stop him. Before

1641 the king could raise money on his own authority in many ways; if Parliament denied him money with a view to extracting concessions, he raised it elsewhere. Experience of Charles I's misgovernment forced the Long Parliament to tamper with the traditional constitutional balance, to restrict the king's use of powers which his predecessors had been trusted to exercise at will. To many, however, these restrictions seemed insufficient to protect the people against future abuses of royal power: Charles seemed determined to reassert his authority by force, so they demanded more. From 1641 to 1648, Parliament demanded that it should have a decisive say in his choice of advisers and control of the armed forces. These restrictions and demands stemmed not from a desire for change but from a concern for self-preservation, but they highlighted one serious weakness of the 'ancient constitution': if the king abused his powers to a point where his people could no longer trust him and co-operation was impossible, who was to judge between them? If the interests of king and people proved irreconcilable, whose came first?

As Parliament struggled to justify making war on the king – legally treason – it was driven to take its stand on its representative function, which implied that authority ultimately derived from the people. This was an implication which many Parliamentarians tried hard to evade or restrict, since it implied that the people should direct their representatives in Parliament, which smacked of democracy. It was therefore argued that, once elected, MPs were not mandated delegates, but free agents, who should make up their minds on each issue on the basis of what they heard in debate. Some of Parliament's more radical supporters, however, had no qualms about locating sovereign power firmly in the people. The Levellers tried to give this concept concrete form by proposing a new constitution which would originate, literally, in the agreement of the people.

Such arguments did not go unanswered. Some Royalist writers began to develop the full implications of the traditional commonplace that royal power came from God. Kings derived their powers from God and were answerable only to God. Government was a matter for the king alone. If he abused his powers, his subjects had no resort other than prayers and tears. To resist the king actively was to resist God – sacrilege. Such ideas were not unknown before 1640: they were expounded by some Laudian divines and James I had made it clear that, while he would obey the laws, this was a matter of choice, a mark of his goodness to his people: he could not be forced to do so. Now they were developed more rigorously.

The comfortable platitudes of the ancient constitution, the reassuring belief that the powers of the Crown and the rights of the subject naturally complemented one another, already under strain before 1640, fell apart during the civil wars. It had been possible to avoid awkward questions about the origins of government by claiming that the king's powers and the people's liberties both dated back to time immemorial and were, like the rest of creation, expressions of the will of God. Now two opposing views of government confronted one another, one of which gave primacy to the wishes and safety of the people, the other to the God-given authority of the king [108; 131].

The emergence of political arguments based on the sovereignty of the people posed an implicit threat to the restored regime, as conservative writers were quick to point out. Much of their response was defensive. Aspects of royal power which had been taken for granted were forcefully and explicitly restated, because they had recently been challenged. Acts were passed stating that the king alone should direct the militia and that the two Houses could not legislate without him. Fearful of the danger from radicals and republicans, speakers in positions of authority went out of their way to stress the divine attributes of kingship and the subject's duty of non-resistance [57] [*Doc. 22*]. Their obvious concern has led historians to argue that the ideas developed in 1640–60 fatally weakened the monarchy's ideological foundations [131].

But did they? Those living in a parliamentary democracy are likely to find the ideas of Parliamentarians and Levellers more familiar and congenial than those of the proponents of divine-right monarchy. It is far from clear that those who mattered politically in Charles II's England felt the same. The reimposition of censorship and the government's tampering with the mails inhibited the expression of unorthodox political views, but it still seems that, however much they have fascinated historians, the ideas of the Levellers and their like won only limited support in their own day. The ruling elite seems largely to have accepted that hierarchy and authority in state and society were interdependent: divine-right monarchy and an aristocratic social order went naturally together.

Restoration Englishmen were not faced with a stark choice between royal absolutism and popular sovereignty. Many, probably most, Royalists in the 1640s shied away from the absolutist implications of divine-right theory and continued to expect the king to respect his subjects' legal rights. From 1642 the king took his stand on the ancient constitution and was probably more scrupulous than Parliament in respecting legal forms. It should be stressed that it was Charles I who had exposed the weaknesses of the old ideal of the mixed and balanced constitution; once he was dead, his successor could be given the benefit of the doubt and the ideal itself remained attractive. By taking away the king's power to levy taxes without Parliament's consent, the legislation of 1641 had altered the balance of power between king and Parliament; events since 1641 suggested that the main priority was now to guard against the threat of revolution from below, by strengthening the king's power to suppress disaffection.

Within the context of belief in the ancient constitution and divine-right monarchy, while accepting that government was the king's business and that active resistance was inadmissible, it was still possible to criticise abuses of royal power without undermining the king's authority or suggesting that it originated in the people's consent [51]. In the words of Sir Orlando Bridgeman:

> Though this is an absolute monarchy, yet this is so far from infringing the people's rights that the people, as to their properties, liberties and lives, have as great a privilege as the king. It is not the sharing of government that is for the liberty and benefit of the people; but it is how far they may have their lives and liberties and estates safely secured under government. [142 *p. 992*]

In the 1640s there had been a ferment of discussion about the origins and nature of government. For much of Charles II's reign there was relatively little. There were frequent arguments about the way the king used his authority in particular cases, but the foundations and legitimacy of that authority were rarely questioned. This was partly because the restored monarchy was so generally accepted, partly because to discuss the origins of government revived unpleasant memories of the civil wars. Even when the Exclusion Crisis raised such issues, by implication, the Exclusionists (in Parliament at least) tried hard to avoid discussing them [*Doc. 33*] [94]. Only in the debates about the change of ruler in 1689 did the Whigs lose their inhibitions and get down to basics.

While it may seem to historians that the new political ideas of 1640–60 ought to have weakened the restored monarchy, there is little hard evidence that they did so. If anything, the reverse seems likely. The reaction against the world's being turned upside-down explains the re-establishment of monarchy on traditional lines, with a large, independent revenue; but (as we have seen) Parliament would not trust Charles too far or give him the means to abuse his authority. Its members wanted him to rule as his predecessors should have ruled – wisely, responsibly and in the best interests of his people.

THE WEAKNESSES OF THE RESTORATION SETTLEMENT

These discussions of the Restoration settlement have so far emphasised the potential strength of the restored regime. It could equally be argued that it had serious structural weaknesses [67; 114; 116]. The problems inherent in the ancient constitution had been dodged. In particular, there was still no mechanism for judging between king and subjects if their interests proved incompatible.

Some political writers in Stuart England were familiar with the concept of sovereignty: in each state there had to be a single ultimate source of law and of political authority. England, however, had a three-part legislature (king, Lords and Commons) and the ancient constitution gave pre-eminence to neither king nor people. The multiple legislature might not seem to be a problem. If a bill could not win the approval of all three partners in the process, then it would not pass. But what if the king, or the king and Lords, refused to pass a bill which the Commons judged to be vital for the people's safety, as had happened in 1641 and was to happen again in 1680? This in turn raised the question of the origins and purposes of government. Did authority originate with God or the people? If the king's powers (or the royal family's rights) seemed incompatible with the people's safety, which should take precedence? Again, these questions had arisen in 1640–2 and were to arise again in 1679–81.

In the 1640s these questions had been resolved, though not definitively, by civil war. However, many had become involved in that war only with extreme reluctance and the experience of the war and its aftermath virtually ruled out rebellion as a viable option after 1660: indeed, in both 1640 and 1688, unpopular English regimes were toppled by outside intervention, not by domestic revolt. That being so, the people, or rather Parliament, had to use more peaceful forms of pressure to keep the king on the straight and narrow. If persuasion was to be effective, Parliament had to be in session; it would be more effective if it was backed up by the power to give or withhold money. In 1641 the Long Parliament had given priority first to ensuring regular parliaments and then to making the king financially dependent on itself by stripping him of his non-parliamentary revenues and voting him taxes for short periods. At the Restoration, the Triennial Act was replaced by an unenforceable measure which no longer stipulated that sessions should last for at least fifty days. Parliament also voted the king revenues, for life, which were supposed to be sufficient to support the government in peacetime.

In 1689 many saw the Restoration revenue settlement as a mistake: 'If king Charles II had not had that bounty from you he had never attempted what he had done' [12 IX *p. 125*]. For Parliament to divest itself of the coercive powers it had acquired in 1641 was a leap of faith which proved to be unwise. It was all the more unwise in that the rise of Louis XIV's France, and his apparent aspirations to universal monarchy, served to sustain the fear of international Popery which had proved so powerful, and divisive, earlier in the century, as well as reviving fears of royal absolutism [67; 114; 115].

All this assumes, however, that it was inevitable that Charles II would misuse his authority, provoke distrust and become embroiled in serious conflict with Parliament. But was it? If Charles matched up to the expectations of the Cavalier Parliament, he would be able to enjoy considerable discretion and exercise substantial power, with little fear of controversy or disorder. If he seemed to threaten the constitutional balance, if he wilfully ignored those political expectations, there was likely to be trouble – although what form that trouble would take remained uncertain. Everything depended on Charles's skills as king and politician and his willingness to confine himself to the politically feasible. In the last analysis, whether one sees the Restoration regime as viable or fatally flawed depends on how one views the Stuarts. For much of the reigns of Elizabeth and James I the ancient constitution functioned tolerably well (as, usually, did the extraordinarily cumbersome constitution of the Dutch Republic). Charles I rendered it unworkable, as did James II. Charles II threatened to do so, but recovered to take the Stuart monarchy to the zenith of its power. In the process he made mistakes – but was it inevitable that he would do so?

CHARLES II: KINGSHIP AND OBJECTIVES

At this point, one should remember the advantages and disadvantages of hindsight. In building up a broadly based impression of opinion within the ruling elite and in Parliament, a historian has access to a far wider range of sources than Charles II had. He had a rudimentary administrative and intelligence-gathering system [92]. He attended some debates in the Lords, but none in the Commons, and relied on second-hand accounts of their supposedly secret proceedings. Whereas now the media offer copious information on political events and attitudes, under Charles II the press was censored and politicians felt less need to justify their conduct to a wider public. Charles's information on politics was, therefore, deficient.

Charles's understanding of politics was also distorted by misconceptions about his subjects. He had been twelve in 1642. He had grown up amid the turmoil of civil war and the uncertainty of exile. In trying to explain his father's execution he looked back beyond Pride's Purge and the rise of the New Model to the civil war itself. Although most Parliamentarians had not wished to abolish the monarchy or to kill the king, one could with hindsight see their making war on him as leading inexorably to his execution. It would also seem logical that the roots of regicide should lie in a disaffection far more widespread than that of the few army officers and Rumpers who brought it about.

Thus, while the historian can argue that the great majority of Charles II's subjects were loyal to the monarchy, one can understand why he should have believed otherwise. His distrust was reinforced by the sometimes ill-tempered disputes and criticism in Parliament, which he (and others) were all too ready to explain in terms of disaffection [*Doc. 19*].

Some have claimed that Charles inclined towards 'absolutism'. In Louis XIV's regime, the concentration in the king of authority and decision-making facilitated the more effective mobilisation of resources for war. It certainly impressed Charles and in an ideal world he might have liked to imitate it. There is, however, little evidence that he seriously intended to make England's government like that of France. Absolutism had evolved in response to specifically French conditions. France had a far more complex and cumbersome administration than England, with great variations between provinces, which made it very difficult to establish effective control over them and to use their wealth and manpower in war. In order to overcome local and corporate vested interests, royal officials developed harsh, authoritarian methods, which they justified by means of an authoritarian political and legal theory. They developed these methods, not in pursuit of any theoretical model of government, but in response to pressing practical needs. France was partially surrounded by the territories of the French kings' inveterate rivals, the Habsburgs. This 'encirclement' created a constant threat of war and forced the Crown to raise all the men and money it could from its diverse and recalcitrant territories. Its efforts were eagerly abetted by officials whose power and profits were enhanced by the extension of royal authority.

Both the problems and the state apparatus of the English Crown were smaller. England's island position allowed it, to a large extent, to opt out of European politics. Its regular military commitments were small – defending the Scots border and maintaining English rule in Ireland – and the former was no longer necessary under Charles II. It did not need a standing army or (thanks to the tradition of local self-government) a large bureaucracy. Institutionally, England was much more integrated than France. Governed as a nation for centuries, it had a single system of law and local government and a single national representative institution. France had a multiplicity of legal systems and retained some provincial representative bodies, or estates; the national Estates General did not meet between 1614 and 1789.

Stuart Englishmen saw in Parliament the embodiment of the difference between the English and French constitutions. Over the centuries, English kings had found it easier to get taxes paid and laws obeyed if they sought the consent of their leading subjects. This reliance on consent was a product of the kings' weak means of coercion, but also served to perpetuate that weakness. Where French kings relied on authority and force, the English sought consent and co-operation at every level, from Parliament to parish. This seemed to foreign observers a feeble and inefficient form of government, but it worked quite well, partly because of the responsibility and public spirit of much of the ruling elite, partly because the Crown's demands were usually small. A large bureaucracy and standing army made for a high level of taxation, with troops and officials needed to collect it. The English Crown found it hard to raise enough money to fight a major war, but after 1689 it became clear that it could, if Parliament was committed to it.

Given the institutional differences between the two countries, it would have been unrealistic and irrelevant to consider establishing 'absolutism' in England. Louis XIV's success owed much to the fact that the ruling elite and the king's officials generally accepted the principles of absolutism. There was no such acceptance in England. Charles II's officials were careful to keep within the law and few, if any, of the ruling elite would have accepted that he could tax or legislate without consent [98].

On the other hand, Louis XIV was able to exact obedience largely because he kept within certain political limits. He respected the privileges of the nobility and the vested interests of his officials and treated his subjects more fairly than his predecessors had done. Here he had much in common with Charles II. Successful kingship depended on making the best use of existing institutions, within limits set by the need to retain the support of the 'political nation'.

Thus for Charles II, had he appreciated it, the problem was to exploit the surge of feeling in favour of monarchy after the civil wars, so as to build up his revenues and maintain peace and order at home. Parliament might vote more revenue for war or if it judged that such revenue was required for good government, it might marginally strengthen his means of coercion if it feared disorder, but the Crown's powers could be increased only with the support of a substantial part of the ruling elite. As one of Charles's ministers wrote: 'Till the king can fall into the humour of his people, he can never be great' [41 II *p. 70*; 51; 98] [*Doc. 23*].

For the king to build upon his subjects' support required mutual trust, but Charles was not disposed to trust them. Bitter experience had left him wary and cynical. A deep sense of insecurity permeated his view of politics and may also have influenced his foreign policy. His fondness for France and hostility to the Dutch perhaps owed something to economic considerations, although by the 1670s France had emerged as an equally serious commercial and colonial rival. Charles also preferred, on principle, France's monarchy to Dutch republicanism and wanted revenge for the destruction of his fleet in the Medway in 1667. Above all, however, Louis had a large army and, until 1673, the Dutch did not. Charles cherished visions of seizing part of the Spanish empire – perhaps even all of Spanish America – when the sickly and childless Carlos II died. For this he would need a powerful ally – and French military aid might also prove useful in case of domestic revolt [93].

Charles's insecurity led him, at times, to conciliate the Dissenters and reinforced his liking for France. Such policies created distrust and resentment, but they were not the only cause of his difficulties with Parliament. He believed his ministers pursued their own interests, rather than his. Had he been prepared to put in the necessary effort, he might have controlled them by checking on their recommendations. As he could not be bothered to do so, he tried to balance individuals and factions, so that nobody gained a monopoly of favour. In 1662–3 he continued to place considerable trust in Clarendon despite his favour to Bennet and Bristol, while in his last years he kept Halifax in office although he was at odds with his fellow-ministers. Such rule by faction could work if the factions' rivalry was kept within limits of discipline and decorum. No such limits existed at Charles II's court, which was frivolous, promiscuous and chaotically informal. Charles was as ready to receive political advice from personal servants as from senior ministers, especially if they made it amusing. He did little to stop courtiers carrying their feuds into Parliament and seems not to have understood the possible dangers of their doing so [*Docs. 24, 25, 26*].

THE WATERSHED OF 1672

The parliamentary history of the reign divides into two distinct phases, with a watershed around 1672. Before then, court faction did much to sour and unsettle the king's relationship with the Commons. Bristol and Bennet's efforts to undermine Clarendon disrupted the session of 1663. With the loss of the fleet in the Medway in 1667 Clarendon's enemies saw a new chance to unseat him. They were led by Bennet, now Earl of Arlington, and the second Duke of Buckingham, whose ability to amuse the king was exceeded only by his lack of political principle and direction. They convinced Charles that the only way to prevent a major crisis when Parliament met was to dismiss Clarendon. When Charles did so, they went further and argued that only Clarendon's death would satisfy the Commons.

The king was persuaded. While the Commons showed only a limited interest in Clarendon's impeachment, Charles canvassed the Lords, urging them to condemn his most loyal servant. Rarely does one see so clearly the self-centred ruthlessness behind Charles's affable façade: to save his skin, he would sacrifice anyone, no matter how innocent.

When Clarendon fled into exile, Arlington and Buckingham turned on his followers. Supported by ambitious MPs kept out of office by Clarendon, they encouraged the Commons to investigate the mismanagement of the Dutch War, hoping to drive out of office those in the financial and naval administration who were protégés of Clarendon and his son-in-law, the Duke of York (who was Lord Admiral). They also revived the idea of making the Church more comprehensive and of granting toleration to Dissenters, mainly because most of Clarendon's followers were committed Anglicans.

Arlington and Buckingham convinced Charles that the Dissenters were more numerous and powerful than the Anglicans and that the Commons would now agree to changes in the Church.

The Commons reacted to the investigation into misgovernment and to the attempts to weaken the Church in very different ways, but each caused rancour and turmoil. Backbenchers, always ready to suspect corruption and incompetence in high places, eagerly supported the investigation, but the majority were committed to the Church of England, and the Commons responded to the proposals in favour of Dissent with new bills against conventicles. Suddenly, early in 1670, Charles dropped his support for concessions to Dissent. The Commons, delighted, voted extra duties on wines for eight years. They lost enthusiasm for the investigation into mismanagement after Charles told them that he could find no evidence that anything was amiss. Soon afterward, he assented to a new conventicle bill [*Doc. 27*].

After the storms of the past few years the sessions of 1670–1 were harmonious and constructive, which showed that if the king gave the Commons the policies they wanted, they would respond positively and even generously [93, 135]. Despite Charles's politically perverse determination to favour Dissent, despite the immorality, corruption and factionalism of his court, the Commons was still ready to believe in the basic integrity of his government. They might haggle about how much money to grant and how to raise it, but usually voted something in the end. They might dislike some of his policies, some aspects of his style of government, but saw no reason to doubt that he would maintain the constitutional balance re-established at the Restoration.

After 1672, this was no longer so. The composition and basic attitudes of the Commons had hardly changed, but developments at court shattered beyond recall the trust between Crown and Parliament which had survived the 1660s. The rest of the reign was to be unsettled by fears that the king and his advisers wished to establish 'Popery and arbitrary government' [*Doc. 28*].

In 1667 the Dutch made peace with Charles because they feared French expansion into the Spanish Netherlands – roughly present-day Belgium – which acted as a buffer-zone between France and the Dutch Republic. In 1668 the Dutch, England and Sweden signed the Triple Alliance, intended to stop France expanding to the north. No sooner had Charles signed it than he began to seek a closer liaison with France. His duplicity and his refusal to confide fully in any of his advisers make it impossible to be certain about his motives. In

May 1670 he signed the Secret Treaty of Dover, in which he agreed to join with France in attacking the Dutch and to declare himself a Catholic. In return, Louis would pay him a subsidy and provide military aid if his conversion provoked disorder.

It is difficult to find a convincing explanation for Charles's promise to announce his conversion, but it is unlikely that he was sincere [65; 78; 93]. In a sense, his motives are unimportant, as the promise remained secret and he showed no sign of acting on it. Of much more immediate political importance was the Anglo-French attack on the Dutch in 1672. Many Englishmen saw Louis as incorrigibly aggressive: once he had overrun the Spanish Netherlands and Dutch Republic, he would turn on England. His demand for freedom of worship for Dutch Catholics gave a religious dimension to the war and it seemed ominous that Charles was taking the 'Catholic' side.

Such anxieties were compounded by Charles's Declaration of Indulgence of March 1672, in which he claimed that his ecclesiastical prerogatives entitled him to suspend the laws against Dissenters, license them to open meeting houses and allow Catholics to worship freely in their homes. This declaration went some way to earning the money which Louis had paid for Charles's conversion and was intended to reduce the danger of the Dissenters making trouble during the war. It provoked alarm for several reasons. The claim that the king could suspend religious statutes might be extended into a claim to suspend any law. Some resented the liberty granted to Dissenters, others the concessions to Catholics. It was even alleged that, as Catholics did not need licences, they were granted a greater freedom than Dissenters [93].

A third development was a growing awareness that the Duke of York had become a Catholic. Despite his many bastards, Charles had no legitimate children, so York was still his heir presumptive. When he failed to take Communion at Easter 1672 tongues began to wag. The prospect of a Catholic king was alarming. English Protestants saw Catholicism as both theologically wrong and a malign political force. Papists were thought to be forever plotting against Protestant rulers, urged on by priests eager for temporal power and popes seeking universal dominion. Once in power they would not rest until, with implacable cruelty, they had rooted out Protestantism. James's conversion seemed doubly threatening in the light of other developments. The Indulgence showed undue favour to Papists and sought to extend the royal prerogative. And why should Charles choose this time to join with the champion of Popery and absolutism to attack a Protestant state? Everything seemed to point to a design to bring in 'Popery and arbitrary government', involving James, and perhaps Charles as well. Once the Dutch had been defeated, the French army would be free to help in this design: some British regiments were already in the French service. The war also provided a pretext to raise an army at home. Many people – even the soldiers themselves – expressed anxiety about the use to which this army might be put [*Doc. 29*].

A deep distrust thus underlay the Commons' aggressive, even hysterical behaviour in 1673. They agreed to give money for the war, but delayed passing the necessary bill until Charles withdrew the Declaration of Indulgence. Later, their refusal to vote any more money forced Charles to make peace with the Dutch early in 1674. When York married an Italian Catholic (his first wife having died) the Commons demanded that the marriage should not be consummated. (York had two daughters, both Protestants, by his first wife. If he now had a son, who would take precedence over them in the succession, he would presumably be brought up as a Catholic, which raised the prospect of a succession of Catholic kings, even if Charles outlived James.) The court was rent with panic and recriminations; politicians sought to divert the Commons' anger on to their colleagues [*Doc. 26*]. Charles, usually so cocksure and cynical, consulted an astrologer about the most propitious time to call Parliament.

DANBY, EXCLUSION AND THE GROWTH OF THE PARTY

In time the panic passed. The war ended and the new army units were disbanded. Charles found a new adviser, Lord Treasurer Danby, who tried to increase the royal revenue and to appeal to the old Cavaliers in the Commons [*Doc. 30*]. After consulting the bishops, he initiated action against Popery and Dissent and sought to restrict public office to firm Anglicans. In so doing, he brought the Church and clergy into the forefront of political controversy, exacerbating divisions between hardline Anglicans and those opposed to the persecution of Dissent; these included not only Dissenters, but those hostile to clerical power and the quasi-absolutist political teachings of some of the clergy and those who regarded Popery as a far greater danger than Dissent [61; 69 Ch. 4]

Danby was accused, justifiably, of re-opening the divisions of civil war: a number of by-elections in the mid-1670s, most notably in

Norfolk, revealed a depth of partisan division which had not been apparent earlier. Meanwhile, Danby used a variety of rewards – places, pensions, preferential treatment at the Treasury – to build up a 'court' party in the Commons. Not only was this seen as further evidence of 'corruption'; it also threatened to undermine the independence of Parliament and so reduce its ability, or will, to oppose the perceived threat of absolutism. For this reason, Danby was accused (by Marvell) of promoting Popery and arbitrary government [41; 69 Ch. 4].

The effect of Danby's policies was to deepen political divisions and to increase distrust of the court. This distrust, reinforced by Charles's reluctance to break with France and James's obvious Catholicism, reduced the effectiveness of his appeal to the Cavaliers. When, in 1678, Charles finally agreed to join with the Dutch against France, many claimed that this was merely a pretext to raise an army. While this army was still in being, Titus Oates's story of a Popish Plot added to the fear of Popery. Shortly afterwards, Danby fell from power and the Cavalier Parliament was dissolved. For the first time since 1661 the electors were to have their say.

Between the spring of 1679 and the spring of 1681 there were three general elections. They revolved around a number of issues: corruption at court, the relationship between Church and Dissent, fears of Popery and arbitrary government. Increasingly, however, the issue of the succession occupied centre stage. The Popish Plot gave a new urgency to the problem of the 'Popish successor': what if the Papists had managed to kill the king? Although there were other possible options, attention focused on moves to exclude York from the succession. Three bills to that effect were introduced into Parliament; one was rejected by the Lords, the other two were lost when Parliament was dissolved. The supporters of exclusion (who by 1681 were coming to be called Whigs) argued that James's religion would inevitably lead him to impose Popery and absolutism by force. Their opponents, the Tories, argued that it was unjust to condemn James untried and that the Whigs' real aim was to start another civil war and overthrow Church and monarchy. While the Whigs denounced the Tories as 'Papists' and 'favourers of Popery', the Tories alleged that the Whigs were scheming republicans who were not really concerned about Popery at all [88; 97] [*Doc. 31*].

At this point, we must address the vexed question of the nature of 'party' in this period [67; 69; 88; 114]. As we have seen, the Restoration settlement failed to address certain key constitutional questions, raised but not resolved in the 1640s: most notably, which took precedence – the rights of the Crown or the safety of the people? These questions arose again over exclusion in 1679–81, while the issue of the Church's relationship with Protestant non-conformity and fears of Popery and arbitrary government again arose in an acute form. There was thus a continuity of issues from the civil wars to Charles II's reign, which in turn made for a continuity in the nature of party divisions, which was exacerbated in the 1660s by 'Cavalier' resentment of the allegedly excessive favour shown to Parliamentarians. Contemporaries were well aware of this, using terms like 'the old Cavaliers', 'the loyal party', 'the king's old friends', 'the factious' and 'the disaffected', all of which harked back to the civil wars. (Alternatively, they spoke of 'the church party' and 'the fanatics', which had similar resonances.) It should be noted that all this labelling was done by Anglican Royalists: their opponents had no wish to perpetuate memories of civil war, but that did not alter the fact that they took a stance similar to that of their Parliamentarian forebears.

Not all political divisions could be fitted into this neat dichotomy, for three reasons. First, Charles often failed to follow the policies which his self-styled supporters expected. This was seen most strikingly in religion, where he persistently promoted comprehension and indulgence. This led to a reversal of normal stances. The opponents of the persecution of Dissent defended the king's use of his prerogative to help Dissenters, while staunch Churchmen, normally defenders of the prerogative, argued that the king was strictly bound by Acts of Parliament.

Second, there were some issues which cut across the essentially ideological divisions outlined above and instead set 'country'* against 'court'. Backbench MPs – whether or not they were country gentlemen – distrusted the corrupt ways of courtiers and civil servants and watched vigilantly for evidence of waste, mismanagement and the abuse of power. The failures of the Dutch War of 1665–7, especially the Medway débâcle, led to demands that those responsible be identified and punished. Often, as in 1663, the backbenchers were egged on by politicians eager to discredit their rivals and drive them out of office. In the 1670s, as we have seen, fear of popery and dislike of Danby's methods of parliamentary management cut across his attempts to build up a 'court' party, based on the Church and old Cavalier interest. In other words, there were two axes of politics, one predominantly ideological (religious and political), the other based on 'country' suspicion of the court. With the growing polarisation from the late 1670s, the two divisions increasingly seemed to coincide, but this was markedly less true earlier on.

Third, amidst all the talk of 'parties', many MPs, and others, tried to avoid blatant partisanship, which was divisive and destructive of neighbourliness and social harmony. Moreover, many still believed that it was possible to combine respect for the king's authority with concern for the liberty and property of the subject. While there were some who espoused the more extreme ideological positions developed during the Interregnum, they were relatively few, most occupying a position nearer the middle of the political spectrum. In the 1670s there is greater evidence of partisan divisions and the polarisation became more marked still in 1679–81.

Quite how this came about and how far it extended is not entirely clear: it is much easier to sketch out ideological positions than it is to measure opinion. The propaganda campaigns from 1679 onwards played a major role, especially once the Tories overcame their reluctance to appeal for mass support. Equally significant were those occasions when an individual was forced to declare publicly where he stood: in votes on exclusion (division lists circulated widely), in elections (votes were given in public) and in signing Whig petitions or Tory loyal addresses (some of which were printed). A growing social segregation developed, with taverns, coffee-houses and clubs becoming identified with a particular party, all of which helped transmit party divisions further and further down the social scale [67; 68; 88]. The net result was that government ministers and local political bosses could identify their friends, and their enemies, with increasing confidence.

The contest over exclusion exposed once more the structural weaknesses of the ancient constitution. James could be excluded only by an Act of Parliament, which needed the consent of king, Lords and Commons. In all three general elections the Exclusionists secured a majority in the Commons, but the king and Lords remained opposed to exclusion. Deadlock ensued, comparable with that in 1641–2 over Strafford's attainder or the militia bill. Again, the Commons' leaders tried to put pressure on the Lords and king by mobilising support outside Parliament, through propaganda, petitions and demonstrations. They urged the king to take the advice of the Commons, which spoke for his people, rather than that of 'evil counsellors'; they claimed that the king's rebuttals of exclusion represented his counsellors' views, not his own. When Charles delayed for fifteen months summoning the Parliament elected late in 1679, they called on him to summon it and allow it to remain in being until all grievances had been redressed, thus (by implication) denying his right to summon and dismiss Parliaments at will. Claiming that James planned a military coup, they demanded the removal of his 'creatures' from the armed forces, thus challenging the king's control of the militia and army. As the Anglican clergy, encouraged by James's promises to stand by the Church, rallied to his defence, the Whigs denounced them as favourers of Popery and demanded toleration for Dissenters, in order to unite all Protestants against the Popish menace.

The Tories took their stand on the defence of 'Church and king'. Again, the political, ecclesiastical and social order seemed to be threatened from below, so the Tories hammered away at the theme of non-resistance. Some perhaps went further than their predecessors in magnifying royal authority. 'All the liberties and privileges the people can pretend to,' wrote Robert Brady, 'were the grants and concessions of the kings of this nation and derived from the crown' [61; 88; 108 *p. 218*]. This implied that the safeguards provided by the law for liberty and property were revocable at the king's pleasure, but the absolutist implications of such arguments were rarely developed and many Tories did not accept them [51] [*Doc. 32*].

If the Tories placed more stress on the king's authority than on the subjects' rights, the Whigs tipped the balance the other way. They emphasised the king's obligation to do what was best for his people and implied that kings existed primarily for their subjects' good. Taken to its logical conclusion this would suggest that the king should agree to whatever his people (as represented in the Commons) thought best, which would reduce his role to that of a figurehead.

Such arguments could be given logical coherence only by arguing that the Commons derived their authority from their representing the sovereign people, but this most Whigs refused to do. As aristocratic as the Tories, the Whig leaders believed that the landed elite should rule. Moreover, arguments for popular sovereignty were associated with the upheavals of 1640–60, which few Whig leaders were prepared to justify – in public, at least. The Whigs were therefore reduced to claiming that although constitutionally the king was free to make up his own mind, he had a moral obligation to satisfy his subjects by agreeing to exclusion. Meanwhile, they put pressure on him to agree, relying mainly on exploiting the popular fear of Popery so as to create the impression that a major revolt might ensue if exclusion were not granted [97] [*Doc. 33*].

THE TORY REACTION

In the Exclusion Crisis the Tories claimed monotonously that ' '41 is here again'. In the sense that it meant a renewed polarisation of the political nation, they were right. The political arguments and electoral mud-slinging created lasting bitterness. In other ways, the similarities were superficial. Civil war was unlikely, partly because Scotland and Ireland largely remained quiet, partly because memories of the 1640s acted as a deterrent, partly because the fears exploited by the Whigs were less intense. In order to scare the king into agreeing to exclusion, they exaggerated the scale and commitment of their popular support. It was one thing to vote for candidates who supported exclusion, but quite another to rebel in order to achieve it.

The fears people felt in 1680–1 were far less immediate than those of 1640–2. They were concerned about how the king's possible successor might behave, if he became king; Londoners took to the streets in 1641–2 because they feared that the king's soldiers might slaughter them or the cannon in the Tower reduce their houses to rubble. This lower level of immediacy in the Exclusion Crisis helps explain the almost total lack of violence until the last months of 1681, when the Whig cause was already lost [66; 97].

Given his fear of rebellion, it was natural that Charles should see the Whigs as republicans: once they had got his brother out of the way, they would destroy the monarchy and himself. He refused to agree to exclusion and played for time, allowing Parliament to investigate the Plot but avoiding substantive concessions. Meanwhile, the panic created by the Plot subsided, the Tory backlash gathered strength, and his ministers ordered his finances so that, when he dissolved the Oxford Parliament of March 1681, he could be confident of surviving without Parliament.

At the Restoration Charles had been reluctant to throw his weight behind the old Cavaliers, but now he appealed unequivocally to his 'old friends', the Tories. They did not disappoint him. In the early 1680s the Crown and the Tories worked together to crush the Whigs and Dissenters. Whigs lost their posts as JPs and in the militia. In many towns, the Tories sought to oust the more active Whigs from the corporation, often by procuring a new charter from the Crown, which gave the king power to remove members of the corporation at will. The commissions appointed under the Corporation Act had been temporary: after they had completed their work, Dissenters and other 'disaffected' persons had slipped back into office [*Doc. 34*]. Under the new charters, the disaffected could be removed at any time.

Often chicanery and undue pressure were used to induce corporations to surrender their charters, but this did not worry the Tories if it produced the desired results – municipal power vested in 'loyal' men and the laws against political and religious dissent effectively enforced. Not all Whigs were excluded from office, in county or town, but those who remained were in a minority and were expected not to oppose the Tories' wishes [60; 95; 105]. Before the new charters of the 1680s, there were many boroughs where Dissenters worshipped in defiance of the laws and Whigs accused of political offences escaped scot-free. The most important was London, whose inability to defend its charter against legal attack led other towns to surrender theirs without a struggle.

The polarisation of the political nation encouraged a politicisation of justice: ' 'Tis now come to a civil war not with the sword but law, and if the king cannot make his judges speak for him he will be beaten out of the field' [4 1680–1, *p. 660*]. The judiciary became solidly Tory; Tory sheriffs chose Tory jurors, and the full weight of the law was turned against Whigs and Dissenters, supplemented by extra-legal pressures, such as the denial of poor relief to those who did not attend Anglican services [70].

In 1681–5, Charles II's was perhaps the most authoritarian royal regime of the century. It proved as well able as Charles I's to crush its political enemies, even without prerogative courts. An incidental benefit of the new charters was that when James became king he was able to influence his first parliamentary election far more than Charles I could have done. The roots of this strength were not institutional but political. Unlike Charles I's Personal Rule, the Tory reaction of 1681–5 had the active support of a large section of the political nation: indeed, the government often had to restrain the Tories' enthusiasm. They assumed that the interests of Crown, Church and Tories were indivisible, a natural and logical assumption while Charles lived. Later, James's conduct forced them into a painful reappraisal of their position.

If Charles survived to live out his last years in peace, this owed as much to luck and the monarchy's inherent strength – especially in terms of popular acceptance – as to his own skills as king. For all his cleverness, perhaps over-cleverness, in diplomacy and intrigue, he seems never to have understood or trusted the men who made up the political nation or sat in Parliament. His distrust, frivolity and (despite his cynicism) openness to suggestion led him to embrace unwise and provocative policies. In the words of the Earl of Mulgrave: 'His great dexterity was in cozening himself, by gaining a little one way while it cost him ten times as much in another and by caressing those most who had deluded him the oftenest' [143 *pp. 58–9*]. Despite his folly and irresponsibility, Charles survived. This owed much to his sense of self-preservation and to the fact the 'he was not striving, nor ambitious, but easy, loved pleasures and seemed chiefly to desire quiet and security for his own time' [27 *pp. 112–3*]. In that respect, Charles was well suited to the politically conservative age in which he lived. His brother, who tried to bring about major changes, lost his throne.

6 RELIGION AND IDEAS

THE RESTORATION CHURCH

After the legislation of the 1660s the Church of England was again the established Church, but was in some ways weaker than before. Those refusing to recognise any national Church were now far more numerous. The sheer physical destruction of church buildings and furniture took years to make good and in some cases was never made good at all. The Church's organisation was restored much more quickly. Bishops, deans and chapters regained possession of their lands, new diocesan officials were appointed and visitations and other aspects of diocesan administration resumed.

The Church courts were re-established, but without High Commission and Star Chamber to back them up were only a shadow of their former selves. For a while they strove to resume their old functions, dealing with moral offences as well as wills, marriages and purely ecclesiastical business. On some matters, notably nonconformity, they proved less effective than the secular courts, as the punishments they imposed carried little weight: excommunication carried no spiritual terror for those with no wish to participate in the Anglican Communion. On other matters, they aroused the jealousy of the common lawyers and by the end of the century they were largely confined to cases in which there was no danger of their trespassing on the jurisdiction of the common law courts [63; 133].

The Church courts' diminished role symbolised the re-establishment of lay domination over the Church. Impropriated tithes, confiscated from Royalists and restored to the clergy in the 1640s, were now returned to their lay owners. Convocation, which even in 1640 had claimed to legislate for the Church independently of Parliament, effectively ceased to function after surrendering its right to tax the clergy in 1664. For both legislative and fiscal purposes, the clergy were now fully subject to Parliament.

Conversely, the clergy now acquired the right to vote in parliamentary elections, raising their political profile and increasing the animus of Whigs and Dissenters against them.

If Laud's hopes of reviving the clergy's authority and autonomy were not fulfilled, he would have found other aspects of the Restoration Church more to his liking. Puritan attempts to reform the Prayer-Book services were decisively rejected. Most parish churches had altars, not Communion tables, and parishioners received Communion kneeling, rather than seated. Most, but not all, Anglican clergymen wore a surplice.

One should not, however, see these developments as evidence of a 'triumph of the Laudians' [38]. They were well established features of the Church before Laud came on the scene and reflected a widespread attachment to the Prayer Book which continued throughout the century. Laud may have increased the Church's stress on ritual and ceremony, but in general his efforts had little lasting impact. Whereas some Laudians had emphasised Communion to the exclusion of preaching, their Restoration successors preached long and hard against sin, heterodoxy and unbelief. The clergy's subordination to the laity increased, church interiors and the conduct of services still fell well short of Laud's idealistic standards, and the clergy still had to come to terms with the realities of village life [109; 122].

That said, an element emerged among the clergy after 1660, whose views on the liturgy, the function of the clergy and the role of the Church in society were akin to Laud's. Particularly identified with the University of Oxford, they were forthright proponents of 'Anglican' values, although the term was rarely, if ever, used at this time. By Anne's reign, when they had become known as 'High Churchmen', they were the most vociferous, if not necessarily the most numerous, section of the clergy. As we have seen, this element became politically conspicuous during Danby's ministry. During the Exclusion Crisis, which many interpreted as an attack on the Church as well as the monarchy, clergymen were active in elections and a major driving force behind the growing Tory backlash. In the early 1680s, apart from encouraging persecution, they played a large part in constructing a Tory ideology based on non-resistance and the hereditary succession, which was to prove a source of acute embarrassment to them in 1688–9 [56; 69 Ch. 4; 122].

In a political sense, the restoration of an effective, hierarchical Church was part of the conservative reaction to the civil wars. Many, disillusioned with evangelism and enthusiasm, came to see the merit of a Church which emphasised stability and a set form of service. Pepys's patron, Sandwich, once a Puritan, told him 'that things would not be well while there was so much preaching and that it would be better if nothing but homilies were to be read in churches' [24 I, *p. 271*]. Later, with the growth of heterodoxy and scepticism, the Church could be seen as the guardian of Christian values.

In short, the great appeal of the High Churchmen was that they stood for tradition and stability in a changing world. Yet although they were strong, they were not all-powerful. Many parish clergymen who had kept their benefices throughout the 1640s and 1650s stayed on after 1662. Many of these were moderate conformists, but some were more Puritan in outlook. Presbyterians had, in 1662, to weigh their distaste for ceremonies and old-style prelacy against their commitment to a national Church and their desire not to lose their livings or abandon their parishioners. There remained in the Church some like Ralph Josselin, who in more than twenty years' ministry under Charles II hardly ever wore a surplice. Others, like Baxter, refused to conform but did not see themselves as nonconformists and attended services conducted by the more Puritan clergy of the established Church. The Church remained broad, but with the balance of power swinging in favour of the High Church element.

CHURCH AND DISSENT

The Church's most striking weakness was that large numbers of Dissenters rejected its spiritual and moral authority. Living in an age when religious pluralism is generally accepted, it is not easy to appreciate the arguments for religious uniformity which were so widely supported, especially by High Churchmen. Recent experience in much of Europe suggested that religious divisions within a state bred political confusion. Many also believed that only an effective Church could maintain moral discipline and uphold Christian values, without which society would dissolve into crime, promiscuity and chaos: the conduct of the Ranters and early Quakers reinforced this belief. Nonconformists were seen as guilty of the sins of schism and spiritual pride; they needed, for their own good, to be brought within the wholesome discipline of the Church and made to heed its teachings and to partake of its sacraments. Particularly in the latter part of the reign, sustained persecution of Dissenters went hand in hand with attempts by the Church's leaders to improve pastoral standards in the parishes. The attempt to restore a national Church and to force Dissenters to conform to it was thus motivated by spiritual ideals as well as by social and political conservatism [62; 122].

Whatever the motives behind the attempts to crush Dissent, they failed. Twenty years' unchecked growth had given the sects strength and self-confidence, while the state's apparatus of coercion proved unequal to the task, especially as many JPs sympathised with Dissent or disliked persecution. As fears of Popery grew, many Anglicans felt that Protestants should unite: bills to grant both comprehension and indulgence were introduced in 1680, but did not become law [75; 121; 127].

The fortunes of Dissent under Charles II were mixed. The incidence of persecution varied, some denominations being harassed far more than others [77]. The greatest sufferers were the Quakers. Many conventional Dissenters regarded them as Papists in disguise; most deplored their elevating the authority of the 'inner light' above that of the Bible. The severity of persecution also varied over time: fierce, if patchy, in the 1660s; limited in the 1670s; very severe after 1680. The Indulgence of 1672, allowing for the opening of licensed meeting-houses, offered a breathing-space after the harassment of the 1660s, enabling the Dissenters to increase their numbers, so that they were better able to withstand the persecution of the 1680s. Finally, there were geographical variations. In general, Dissenters worshipped more freely in towns, where the corporation often failed to enforce the laws, than in rural areas, where the magistrates were gentlemen appointed by the Crown. In many towns the laws were rarely enforced until the changes of magistrates in the 1680s [*Doc. 34*].

The relative strength of Anglicanism and Dissent is hard to determine. In 1676, Henry Compton, Bishop of London, organised a religious census. Clergymen were to send in the numbers of Anglicans, Dissenters and Catholics in their parishes. While the figures for Catholics may have been quite accurate for much of the country [97], those for Dissent seem implausibly low [*Doc. 35*]. The aim of the census was to enable Danby to prove to the king that the Anglicans were much the largest religious group, so incumbents were asked to return the numbers of Dissenters 'which either obstinately refuse or wholly absent themselves from the communion of the Church of England' [132 *p. xxix-xxx*]. This would ensure that the many occasional conformists (like Baxter) were returned as Anglicans, as were those whose religious convictions were lukewarm or minimal and who rarely, if ever, attended church (or any other place of worship). At the parish level it was not always easy to distinguish conformists from non-conformists, or to say to which sect the latter belonged [*Docs. 35, 36*] [129; 132].

In a society where the majority of people were illiterate and received no formal education, it is not surprising that the religious understanding of many was limited or that some people's ideas were confused, especially after the recent ferment of debate. Some upland areas remained largely untouched by organised religion, despite the efforts, at different times, of Anglicans, Catholics, Baptists and Quakers [*Doc. 37*]. In general, the Church was strongest in the larger, more compact villages and market towns of the south and Midlands. The main strength of Dissent lay in the larger towns, industrial communities and the more dispersed villages and hamlets of forest, pastoral and upland regions. Catholicism survived in pockets in the south and Midlands, bunched around gentry house-holds, and in remote, hilly areas in the north and the Welsh Marches.

After making due allowance for the inadequacies of the Compton Census, it is clear that Dissenters made up only a minority, and not a very large minority, of the population. One reason for their limited numbers was persecution, but that was uneven in incidence and was often least severe where Dissent was strongest, in towns. Only a minority of English people lived in towns, however, and in rural areas the Anglican gentry, in their dual capacity as landlords and magistrates, could put pressure on people to conform. Dissenting and Catholic landlords did much to sustain the numbers of their denominations [*Doc. 36*], but Dissent soon lost most of its gentry support after 1660 [47] and the Catholic gentry were never very numerous.

It also seems likely that the appeal of Dissent was inherently limited. To belong to a 'gathered church' required a level of spiritual commitment which only a minority possessed: the initial excitement of conversion was often hard to sustain. One had to be tough and confident of one's righteousness to put up with the mutual criticism which many congregations practised. The emphasis of most Dissenters on the Bible as the source of authority would tend to deter the illiterate, although it did not always do so. As a religion of the Word, Dissent involved considerable intellectual effort: sermons could last for hours. For many, probably the great majority, the Church of England, with its set cycle of services and its participation in physical acts of worship, must have seemed intellectually less demanding and spiritually more edifying. It was not given to everyone to be a spiritual athlete.

A final reason for the limited appeal of Dissent can be found, yet again, in the 1640s and 1650s. Laud's fall encouraged apocalyptic hopes of a more perfect spiritual order on earth, a rule of the saints. There were hopes that God Himself would bring this order into being, but if He did so, He worked in mysterious ways. Instead of His guiding the gathered churches towards harmony, they drifted apart amid acrimony. Confident predictions that the world was about to end proved incorrect, while the Ranters' excesses convinced many Puritans that they were heading not for perfection but for chaos.

The frustration of the hopes of the 1640s led to disillusionment. Many conservative Puritans turned to the Church as the only guarantee of order and stability. Most sects, instead of seeking to change the world, turned in on themselves and concentrated on maintaining their own spiritual purity, a development which was encouraged by the onset of persecution. Even the Quakers lost their early aggression and exhibitionism and became quiet and respectable. The once militant proponents of the 'lamb's war' were now at pains to show that they were peaceable, embracing pacifism and eventually ceasing to evangelise. The 'Puritan Revolution' shattered the broad consensus of the early 1640s and made a united Puritan front impossible: at the Restoration, most Presbyterians wanted comprehension, but other Dissenters sought only toleration. It also destroyed the Puritans' self-confidence, their belief that God was with them and that unlimited preaching and debate would produce a more godly and united society. Belief in divine Providence led some to accept the Restoration fatalistically as God's punishment for their sins [*Doc. 9*]. Finally, the excesses of 1640–60 provoked a reaction against 'enthusiasm' among Protestants of all kinds.

LATITUDINARIANISM AND SCIENCE

This reaction was seen most clearly within the Church, among those who were often labelled Latitudinarians. Whatever their disagreements, High Churchmen and Puritans like Baxter dealt in dogmatic certainties, although the former sought authority in the Fathers and the Church's traditions, as well as the Bible, while the latter relied on the Bible alone. This dogmatism led to bitter arguments about such symbolic points as kneeling at Communion and the use of the sign of the cross in baptism. The Latitudinarians declared themselves weary of such wranglings. Surely, they argued, it was more rational and constructive to concentrate on the basic tenets of Christianity, on which all agreed, and on practical morality. Too much fervour clouded the understanding and distracted the clergy from their main task of encouraging people to lead better lives. Taken to extremes, this approach led some to reduce the essentials of Christianity almost to nothing, to develop an essentially functional view of morality (leading a good life was profitable) and to make religion so devoid of emotion as to be deadly dull. Under Charles II, however, they were among the most articulate defenders of the Church against both Dissent and Popery, as well as warning of the dangers of libertinism and atheism. However, once Parliament had granted toleration to Dissenters in 1689, they came to terms with religious pluralism far more quickly than their High Church brethren, while their lack of dogmatism made them more open than High Churchmen or Dissenters to the appeal of science.

It has often been argued that Protestantism, with its stress on the individual's interpretation of the Bible, was more conducive to scientific enquiry than Catholicism, which subordinated individual judgement to the authority of the Church. To some extent this is plausible, but many Protestants rejected scientific ideas which contradicted the teachings of the Bible and most Protestant churches imposed severe restrictions on intellectual freedom. In the second half of the seventeenth century, the most fruitful scientific activity took place in England and the Dutch Republic, where the established Protestant Churches were comparatively weak. In England, scientific debate had flourished in the absence of ecclesiastical authority in the Interregnum and the momentum was not lost at the Restoration. Science became fashionable, in part, because of Charles's patronage of the Royal Society.

For many, an interest in science went little further than idle curiosity. Evelyn described the Royal Society as 'an assembly of many honourable gentlemen who meet inoffensively together, under His Majesty's royal cognizance, and to entertain themselves ingenuously whilst their other domestic avocations or public business deprives them of being always in the company of learned men' [76]. Much of the Royal Society's time was taken up with trivial matters and many 'scientists' amassed information with little idea of how to organise or analyse it. Alongside the dilettantes and eccentrics, however, were serious experimenters and statisticians, and popularisers who believed that scientific knowledge could serve a constructive social purpose: only by accumulating data could one begin to understand the world, and until one understood it one could not begin to improve it.

In terms of practical economic and social improvement, the achievements of Restoration science seem meagre. The Royal Society publicised new crop rotations developed in the Low Countries, but it is uncertain how widely farmers adopted them. It was easier to gather statistics on population or trade than to apply them to the practice of government [45; 76]. Perhaps the most important achievement of the new interest in science was to help to create a mood of optimism, often overstated, about the potential of human knowledge and the possibility of human improvement [*Doc. 38*]. Science offered rational explanations for phenomena once understood in terms of evil spirits or divine wrath – or held out the hope that such explanations could be found. If the universe could be shown in some respects to function according to ascertainable mathematical laws, why not the physical world as well?

This rational approach to the world and the cosmos was potentially at odds with older explanations in terms of either the hand of God or occult forces. Some saw science as a threat to orthodox Christianity, or resented the cavalier way in which some of its proponents dismissed traditional authorities and explanations, but many found little difficulty in reconciling science and religion. Closer inspection of God's creation could increase respect for His achievement. To show that parts of creation obeyed mathematical laws did not necessarily cast doubt on His having established those laws, or on His ability to intervene arbitrarily if He chose. It took time for the belief to spread that God intervened rarely or never in earthly affairs, having created a wonderfully complex set of self-regulating mechanisms which required no further action on His part – and such a belief was never universally accepted.

Belief in occult forces did not disappear either, especially among the less educated, but became increasingly unfashionable among the educated elite. Parliament had passed an Act in 1604 describing witchcraft as a crime against God, as it involved a pact with the devil. In the decades that followed, JPs proved willing to receive accusations of witchcraft and judges and juries were prepared to convict those accused. In the later seventeenth century, however, JPs and judges became noticeably more reluctant and convictions ceased well before the witchcraft laws were repealed in 1736 [*Doc. 39*] [126].

A growing emphasis on a scientific, rational approach served to undermine religious dogmatism and belief in the occult, but only within the educated minority, and even within that many were unaffected or only partly convinced. Some held beliefs which to modern eyes might seem incompatible. Sir Isaac Newton, whose discoveries did much to strengthen the concept of the universe as a self-regulating mechanism, denounced such a concept, was reluctant to deny the possibility of miracles, and dabbled in alchemy. Religious teachings were adapted to take account of new discoveries; occult beliefs continued alongside scientific ideas.

When all qualifications have been made, however, the new science and the reaction against enthusiasm helped to create, among the educated elite, a mentality, an intellectual approach which was substantially different from that of the first half of the century. Religion became less a subject of dogmatic certainty, more a private matter, on which there was room for honest disagreement. The world was no longer seen as irredeemably corrupt, a snare and delusion through which one passed on the way to the perfection of the after-life. Many now saw the world as worthy of study in its own right – and why not, for it was God's handiwork. Growing understanding of the world led to a belief that man might one day be able to make his life happier, more comfortable and more secure. By improving crops and agricultural techniques, more food could be produced. By making better use of a nation's resources (not least its labour force) its wealth might be greatly increased.

Early Stuart writers claimed that England was overpopulated, its resources overstretched; providing for the poor seemed a huge and insoluble problem. By Charles II's reign, some expressed greater optimism. They no longer proclaimed that the end of the world was nigh, nor that mankind was irremediably weak and sinful, nor that life on earth was simply a painful preparation for the perfection and true happiness of the hereafter. They were coming to believe that the world could be improved – in short, in the possibility of progress [45; 126].

PART THREE: ASSESSMENT

7 THE PLACE OF THE RESTORATION IN ENGLISH HISTORY

It is often claimed that the 'English Revolution' permanently altered England, that it brought about (or completed) a seismic change in the structure of society and unleashed new ideas which, with the king's execution, irreversibly weakened the monarchy. Arguments that there were major social changes rest on the premise that the 'Revolution' was itself the product of a long-term process of socio-economic change, a premise which is at best not proven.

The pre-eminence of land in both the economy and society continued throughout the century. Agriculture remained much the largest employer, land remained the largest source of wealth, the quality of the harvest still affected the whole of the economy. In social terms, the continuing importance of the landed elite and of landed values was shown by the eagerness of those who made money in the law and civil service, in trade and finance, to buy country estates and establish themselves as members of the gentry. The structure of society was not to be drastically changed until the structure of the economy was transformed, over a century later, by the Industrial Revolution.

As far as other types of change are concerned, I have suggested that the new radical ideas of the mid-century found little support after 1660 and probably served only to strengthen the conservatism of the ruling elite. The Puritans' victory over Laud was a pyrrhic one: they emerged after 1660 divided, disillusioned and in many ways discredited.

The reaction against the changes of 1640–60 might seem odd, but only if one sees those changes as developing out of the interests and aspirations of the more influential groups in society. If, however, men were forced by circumstances into actions which went against their principles, if they were carried along by events outside their control, the reaction after 1660 becomes far more comprehensible. Most had not wanted civil war, the abolition of monarchy or religious confusion. They had no wish to be ruled by soldiers or to have the world turned upside-down. The Restoration gave a welcome opportunity to return to normal.

Historians have looked hard for ways in which the events of 1640–60 could have weakened the monarchy, but have shown far less interest in ways in which they might have strengthened it. The civil wars and Interregnum saw an unprecedented strengthening of the English state, at the heart of which was a radical reshaping of the fiscal system. Much of the Crown's revenue before 1640 came from its lands (although these were worth less and less as land was sold off) and from an archaic, random assortment of feudal and property rights and regulatory powers which the Crown had accumulated over the centuries and which (as means of raising money) had often proved inefficient, contentious and unfair.

The only major tax revenues which the king received were the customs – normally granted by Parliament to an incoming monarch (though not to Charles I) – and the subsidy. This was also granted by Parliament, when the king could persuade it that it was necessary (for example, for war). It was a property tax, mainly on land. Landowners gave in an account of their income, deducting necessary expenses. They were not on oath, so it was a matter of persuading the assessment commissioners appointed by Parliament, who were often their friends or neighbours, that the valuation was accurate. One result of this was that valuations began to fall under Elizabeth even in money terms and (because of inflation) much more sharply in real terms. By 1628 one subsidy brought in less than half the sum raised in the 1590s, which was in turn less than in the 1560s. This underassessment was partly offset by persuading the Commons to vote two, four or even six subsidies, but generally income from the subsidy became less and less important compared with that from prerogative finance.

Throughout early modern Europe, the emphasis of states' revenues shifted from the exploitation of their feudal and property rights towards taxation (and borrowing secured on the proceeds of taxation). Through taxation they could tap the various forms of their people's wealth and economic activity. In predominantly agricultural economies, this meant the imposition of direct taxes on land – preferably accurately assessed and efficiently collected – and of indirect taxes on various forms of transaction (for example, imports and exports). Measured against these standards, the Tudor and early Stuart revenue system was primitive and inefficient: indeed, the Tudors had survived financially only by plundering the

Church. The only land tax, the subsidy, became less and less effective as a means of tapping wealth and the only other form of economic activity that was taxed was overseas trade. There were no taxes (as such) on goods produced and sold within the country. This also meant that much of the population – those who did not own sufficient property and did not buy imported goods – effectively paid no tax at all (although they might be liable to local rates and pay inflated prices for monopoly commodities) [40].

Before 1642, the Commons showed little concern to reform the tax system. Not only did they not wish to upset their neighbours by increasing taxation, they had little wish to give the early Stuarts the resources they would need to rule without Parliament. In 1642, however, having swept away most of the Crown's domanial revenues, Parliament found itself with only the customs, loans and voluntary contributions to sustain its war effort. For the first time, MPs had a vested interest in raising large sums of money quickly. After hesitating to vote taxes without the king's assent, in 1643 Parliament established two new ones.

The weekly or monthly assessment was a land tax, which got round the problem of underassessment by laying down a quota which each county and town had to meet, so that arguments about assessment would shift the burden between one taxpayer or locality and another, without reducing the overall yield. Ironically, the assessment's quota system was modelled on that of ship money, perhaps the most unpopular of the 'arbitrary' exactions of the 1630s – but it was levied at a much higher rate.

The excise (based on a Dutch model) was levied on a number of commodities produced and consumed within England, including (for a while) meat and salt, but it came to fall most heavily on beer and other alcoholic drinks. It was initially extremely unpopular (which is why the duty on meat was abandoned) but by the 1650s was being levied relatively efficiently with little popular resistance [39; 40; 102].

These two new taxes, along with the customs, gave England, for the first time, a rational, efficient and modern fiscal system. The tax burden on the population increased enormously, but the taxes were paid, partly because they had the authority of Parliament behind them, partly because (as with the subsidy) local people were often involved in assessment and collection, and partly because the more contentious elements (like the meat excise) were abandoned and they were collected in ways which minimised conflict (the beer excise was collected at the brewery rather than in the alehouses). It no doubt helped that the government had an army at its disposal, but troops were rarely used to deal with tax disorders, not least because they were infrequent. Meanwhile, the fact that the yields of these taxes were both substantial and predictable made them good security for loans from the City of London [39; 40].

Charles II inherited a fiscal system far more rational and efficient than his father's, as well as a population becoming accustomed to substantial, regular taxation. Charles's regime built on this foundation, notably by establishing permanent networks of collectors for the customs, excise and hearth tax by the 1680s. Sir George Downing also tried to systematise the Crown's borrowing, but his system collapsed in the Dutch War of 1672 [113].

This new fiscal system was not Charles's only valuable legacy from the Interregnum. If not all the governmental changes of that period survived the Restoration, one sees in the 1660s a greater administrative professionalism: a concept of service to the state was beginning to replace the older view of office as a piece of property, to be exploited for personal profit. Samuel Pepys never disdained an opportunity to make money, but saw the king's service as his first concern. His love of order and method was shared both by old Cromwellians like Downing and by younger men like Charles Davenant, at the Treasury, and William Blathwayt, Secretary at War [35; 128]. The restored monarchy also appreciated the potential benefits of the Navigation Act of 1651. Re-enacted and extended, it contributed to the expansion of English trade and shipping, its enforcement greatly facilitated by another legacy of the Interregnum, a much enlarged navy, with three times as many substantial vessels in 1662 as in 1642 [53].

Thus state-building of 1640–60 offered the potential for a restored monarchy financially and administratively stronger than that of Charles I. To some extent that potential was realised. The navy continued to grow and to enforce the Navigation Acts. Trade and shipping flourished, boosting both the customs and the excise, whose yield was also improved by increasingly efficient and professional management. On occasion, Charles II received grants of taxation which dwarfed those of his predecessors: the £2,500,000 voted in 1664 was about six times as large as the largest grant of the 1620s.

Yet when all is said and done, Charles II did not make the most of this potential. Underlying all else was the question of money. Charles's revenues depended on Parliament. His finance officials duly maximised the yield of the revenues granted him for life at the

Restoration, but he could not obtain further grants, either temporary or permanent, without Parliament's agreement. (The notorious subsidies from Louis XIV made only a small contribution to his income.) This brings us back to a central argument of this book: that Charles II's government was most effective when he secured the co-operation of Parliament and he could do that only when he pursued policies acceptable to Parliament [*Docs. 23, 30*]. Once distrust had set in – notably after 1672 – additional grants of revenue proved harder and harder to come by and he was thrown back on his ordinary revenue. This was not a disaster, but it left him quite unable to contemplate making war. Like his father in the 1630s, Charles II was unable to afford an active foreign policy after 1679. For a king who in the 1660s had had grandiose ambitions of humbling the Dutch and even seizing a large part of the Spanish empire, this was a major comedown. Only after 1689, when king and Parliament again co-operated in financing major wars against the French, was the fiscal and military potential of the English state fully realised.

If Charles II failed to make the most of his opportunities, however, I would suggest that this was not because his regime was inherently weak, a ramshackle structure thrown together in a panic fear of anarchy in 1660. By trying to return to things as they should have been before 1640, the Convention and Cavalier Parliament sought to give permanence to the restored monarchy. If they failed, the reasons should be sought not in any inadequacy of the Restoration settlement, but in Charles II's and James II's failure to understand the practical limits on their conduct, imposed by the interests and prejudices of the political nation. James refused to recognise those limits, and paid the penalty. Charles made many mistakes, but was saved by his lack of ambition and a fundamental instinct for self-preservation.

PART FOUR: DOCUMENTS

DOCUMENT 1   GENERAL MONK

Monk's chaplain describes how he carried his officers and soldiers with him.

The General had ... his great council of all commission officers in the army. It was a pleasant sight to see the General at the end of a table, in a room full of officers, putting the question ... and then an ensign to make a long speech to the contrary (who was but started from a corporal the other day) ... but though he submitted to these forms, yet he kept an absolute authority by the prudence and artifice of those he trusted, but did it by the way of counsel and persuasion, and though he was good at driving, yet he was now forced to lead gently ... The great care that was taken was to catechize the soldiers well, into the principles and first rudiments of their duty and obedience and to spirit them into an understanding and sense of the quarrel; for upon the meeting of the Scottish and English forces in the field, it was supposed ... that they would with difficulty enough be brought to fight one against the other ...

Gumble, [13], pp. 140v–141r.

DOCUMENT 2   THE POLITICAL SITUATION IN
             DECEMBER 1659

The Royalist Allan Broderick tells Hyde that the Royalists cannot exploit their numerical preponderance, and that all depends on Monk. Five days after, he wrote, the Rump reassembled.

To my short-sighted view, the prospect appears thus: no interest in the nation equals that of monarchy, whether we regard the number, wealth, courage or birth of the persons sincerely devoted to it; but the numbers are generally ill-armed, unmodelled, uncounselled, the wealth hoarded up or spent in luxury; the courage entertained with private animosities, and birth extends little further than escutcheons and precedency, save in some few ... The next is the Presbyterian, who would have half a king, half a commonwealth, their numbers declining with the absence of the former; all men growing up since 1646 being of the better sense, besides many worthy converts. The Independents, as they are in congregate churches ... of Anabaptists, Quakers, Seekers, Singers, &c. are three parts women to one of men, whose noise is consequently greater, but effects disproportionate. The army mixed (though very unequally) of all these is united by a general maxim ... of opposing the common enemy, nor do any private petulancies provoke them to forget the public danger, wherein they only exceed us and (almost deservedly) enslave us ...

[As for Monk] his letter to the fleet and his protestations to Cargill (one of those sent to him by the committee of safety) positively assert the Rump. His other discourses and letters seem to aim at the Parliament of 1648. His conference of August last year gives me yet a better hope and what the honest man for his oath's sake concealed will, I hope, break forth with this happy opportunity; a sober man he is, ambitious of a good fame as much as great, though I doubt too much bigot in Presbytery ...

Clarendon State Papers, [6], vol. III, pp. 631–3.

DOCUMENT 3   A PETITION FOR A FREE PARLIAMENT

In January and February 1660 there were petitions, to Monk or the Rump, from at least nineteen counties, for a free Parliament. This is a summary of the Oxfordshire petition, presented to Monk and said to bear over 5,000 signatures.

1. That as they were freeborn people and subjects of England, that it was a privilege that knights and burgesses ought to be present in Parliament for the good of their country [i.e., county] and in many places in the countries are wholly left out, either by death or seclusion.
2. That all places vacant by death may be supplied, and that those that was secluded in 1648 may be a[d]mitted.
3. That no unusual, previous or foreru[nn]ing oath may be put upon any man that is to sit in Parliament, and that no taxes may be put upon us without our free consent in Parliament.
4. That the fundamental laws of the land, the privilege of Parliament, the liberty of the subject, the property of goods may be asserted and defended according to the first declaration of Parliament when they undertook the war.
5. That the true Protestant religion may be professed and defended, a lawful succession of godly and able ministers continued [and] encouraged and the two universities ... preserved and countenanced ...

Rugg, [28], pp. 40–1, corrected against British Library, Add MS. 10116, fo. 60.

DOCUMENT 4   THE RUMP'S DECLARATION, 23 January
               1660

Faced with calls for a free Parliament, the Rump issued this promise of elections, but insisted that only republicans should be eligible to sit. It also gave assurances on other matters.

I. That the Parliament will provide forthwith to perfect those beginnings which are already made for settling the government ... in the way of a commonwealth and free state, without a king, single person or House of Lords, in such manner that they may be governed from time to time by representatives in Parliament chosen by themselves, in whom alone the supreme authority of these nations doth and ought to reside, and by such as they shall appoint and constitute officers and ministers under them for the good of the people; and that the Parliament will make it their care to form the army and forces of these nations in such a manner that, whilst it shall be found necessary for them ... to be kept up for the safety of the commonwealth, they may be wholly subject and obedient to the civil authority ...
II. That all proceedings touching the lives, liberties and estates of all the free people of this commonwealth shall be according to the laws of the land ...
III. And that they will make effectual provision for the countenancing of a learned and pious gospel ministry ... And as to their maintenance, that by tithes shall be continued ... as also that provision shall be made for due liberty of conscience in matters of religion, according to the word of God ...
VI. As to the present burdens which are upon the nation, the Parliament is very sensible thereof ... and it is one of the greatest cares they have upon them how to give the people that ease which their condition calls for ... which the Parliament hopes in some measure to do in a very short time ...

Old Parliamentary History, [23], vol. XXII, pp. 60–2.

DOCUMENT 5   MONK SEEKS TO REASSURE THE ARMY

This is part of a circular in which Monk and his officers try to justify to the rest of the army their having readmitted the MPs excluded in 1648, as the best way to secure a new Parliament 'under such qualifications as may secure our cause'.

And to take away all just jealousies from you, we do assure you that we shall join with you in the maintenance of those ends expressed in the enclosed and do expect your cheerful concurrence with us. And we desire to take God to witness that we have no intentions or purposes to return to our old bondage; but since the providence of God hath made us free at the cost of so much blood, we hope we shall never be found so unfaithful to God and His people as to lose so glorious a cause. But we do resolve, with the assistance of God, to adhere to you in the continuing our dear-purchased liberties, both spiritual and civil. The reasons of our proceedings in this manner may seem strange; but if you duly consider the necessities of our affairs and the present state of things, you will certainly conclude nothing so safe to secure public interest and to engage the nations peaceably to submit to a free state ... and it is the opinion of the truest friends to a free state that it cannot be consistent with the perpetual sitting of these members, being contrary to the nature of such a government ...

Old Parliamentary History, [23], vol. XXII, pp. 170–1.

DOCUMENT 6   THE DECLARATION OF BREDA, 4 APRIL 1660

This removed most of the more immediate anxieties which might lead individuals to oppose the king's return.

And to the end that the fear of punishment may not engage any, conscious to themselves of what is past, to a perseverance in guilt for the future, by opposing the quiet and happiness of their country, in the restoration of king, peers and people to their just, ancient and fundamental rights, we do ... grant a free and general pardon ... to all our subjects ... who within forty days after the publishing hereof shall lay hold upon this our grace; ... excepting only such persons as shall hereafter be excepted by Parliament ... we desiring and ordaining that henceforth all notes of discord, separation and difference of parties be utterly abolished among all our subjects, whom we invite and conjure to a perfect union among themselves, under our protection, for the re-settlement of our just rights and theirs in a free Parliament, by which, upon the word of a king, we will be advised.

And because the passion and uncharitableness of the times have produced several opinions in religion, by which men are engaged in parties and animosities against each other (which, when they shall hereafter unite in a freedom of conversation, will be composed or better understood), we do declare a liberty to tender consciences, and that no man shall be disquieted or called in question for differences of opinion in matter of religion which do not disturb the peace of the kingdom; and that we shall be ready to consent to such an Act of Parliament as, upon mature deliberation, shall be offered to us, for the full granting that indulgence.

And because ... many grants and purchases of estates have been made to and by many officers, soldiers and others, who are now possessed of the same, and who may be liable to actions at law upon several titles, we are likewise willing that all such differences ... shall be determined in Parliament, which can best provide for the just satisfaction of all men who are concerned.

And we do further declare, that we will be ready to consent to any Act or Acts of Parliament to the purposes aforesaid and for the full satisfaction of all arrears due to the officers and soldiers of the army under the command of General Monk; and that they shall be received into our service upon as good pay and conditions as they now enjoy.

Gardiner, [11], pp. 465–7.

DOCUMENT 7   'THE GENERAL'S PAPER'

These proposals, designed to secure the Presbyterians' personal, political and religious interests, were put to Parliament early in May 1660 (see Doc. 12). They show that Monk wished to impose strict conditions on the king.

1. The sales [of confiscated lands] to those now in service in the army and navy ... to be confirmed for ninety-nine years, at the reserved rents not exceeding a sixth of the full yearly value.
2. The sales of bishops', deans' and chapters' and crown lands to other persons, not of the army or navy, to be confirmed for sixty years, at a rent reserved of the fifth part of the yearly value.
3. The sales of lands of all other persons to continue in the purchasers' hands ... till satisfaction be made with interest at six per cent and their charges, as in the case of mortgages. Excepted out of the act of confirmation: the purchases of all persons that sat ... in the high court of justice for the trial of the late king or in the council of safety [also certain other exceptions].
4. The annulling of all things passed under any Great Seal since 22 May 1642, except the seal appointed or used by authority of Parliament.
5. That of the Acts and Ordinances passed by the late Parliament, the king confirm such as both Houses shall tender unto him; particularly to pass an Act taking away the court of wards upon the recompense of £100,000 per annum ...
6. Excepted persons in the Act of Oblivion: [five of those actively involved in the king's trial].
7. The General to have the command of the army during life.
8. The exercise of the Protestant religion and ministry to continue in the same state as now they are, until an assembly of divines shall be called, so that thereby, with the Parliament, the government of the Church may be settled.

Lister, [17], vol. III, pp. 500–1.

DOCUMENT 8   REACTIONS TO THE RESTORATION:
                  THOMAS RUGG

*Rugg was a London barber whose 'Diurnal' is a mixture of extracts from
newsbooks, gossip and his own thoughts.*

Now the state of affairs began to appear barefaced, and the truly noble
English spirit to be visible in the restoration of our most famous Charles II
... who, having tired envy itself and overcome more difficulties than
humanity could endure, was by a general vogue invited to the exercise of his
kingly office, which, after a long interval of change and foolish endeavours
of new governments, was to the dear cost of the whole nation found to be
the most complete and perfect government that ever bore sway here, under
which may we still live, but with that freedom that we have undergone
slavery in the rest ...

Rugg, [28], p. 87.

DOCUMENT 9   REACTIONS TO THE RESTORATION:
                  EDMUND LUDLOW

*Ludlow, a religious and political radical, tries to come to terms with the fact
that God has apparently abandoned 'the godly' by allowing the Restoration.*

I am assured it was done by the wise disposing hand of God, without whose
providence not a sparrow falls to the ground, much less the blood of any of
His precious saints ... ; whose dispensations herein, as they have been
righteous (in that the nation in general seemed not to be fitted for that
glorious work which He seemed to be doing for them by the means of some
of His poor people ...) so I am confident that these very dispensations will
... appear to be in mercy and peace to His poor people and to all who
desire to live godly in the land, and that when in the furnace they are
melted into one lump, they shall come forth as refined gold. But it's the
Lord's pleasure they should take their turn in the wilderness ... He seems to
take the rod into His own hand to correct them for their disobedience and
unsuitable returns to all those eminent appearances of His amongst them;
Charles Stuart and his party not contributing the least to their restitution ...
Yet so it is that the Lord is pleased for the present to make them the tail,
who before were the head ...

Ludlow, [20], pp. 149–50.

DOCUMENT 10   DISSATISFACTION WITH THE COURT

Of the many expressions of dissatisfaction with the court and with Charles's favour to the Presbyterians, this was perhaps the earliest, dated a week after his arrival in London.

'Tis not to be imagined how many are dissatisfied; innumerable flocks of people hovering here to see how they may light upon places and preferments: the court and royal party grudging at every favour to the Presbyterian, and they on the other side thinking they have not enough, and all that is done to them being wrought by the General [Monk] has begot much murmuring at him; 'tis thought too much that Lord Manchester should be lord chamberlain and four or five others of the privy council, as Holles, Annesley, Mr William Pierpoint, Sir Anthony Ashley Cooper and Mr Secretary Morrice ... and all this the General's doing ... .

Historical Manuscripts Commission, Fifth Report [15], p. 184.

DOCUMENT 11   ATTEMPTS TO LIMIT THE KING'S POWERS

In the weeks before Charles's return, the Presbyterians sought to restrict his powers and schemed to exclude Hyde from office.

By stories artificially related both to the General and his lady, your enemies have possessed them both with a very ill opinion of you ... I look on Manchester as the prime author of this, who is set on from beyond sea [by the queen mother]. I am the more confirmed in this since the message the Lords sent to the Commons to desire them to add Manchester to the others as commissioner of the seal ... Though the legislative power may remain in the king, Lords and Commons, ... the executive was never questioned to be in the king; and though the name may be allowed him, how little that will signify when he parts with the militia I need not say ...

Lord Mordaunt to Hyde, 4 May 1660, Lister, [17], vol. III, p. 100.

DOCUMENT 12   ATTEMPTS TO LIMIT THE KING'S POWERS (continued)

This gives details of the legislation proposed by the Presbyterians and of the Royalists' attempts to thwart them: see also Doc. 7.

A bill was twice read this morning, committed and returned to be engrossed whereby His Majesty makes this a legal Parliament, though the writ was unduly issued. Another for confirmation of all [land] sales till further order or satisfaction by Parliament to the purchasers &c was twice read and committed. A third for arrears of the army and navy is drawn. A fourth for tender consciences, allowing the exercise of religion as now it is, till all controversies be determined by a national synod. A fifth to take away the court of wards, with allowance to His Majesty of £100,000 per annum in lieu thereof ... The last and main bill, for indemnity and free pardon, is in the hands of Serjeant Maynard, who will (if there be any time) report it tomorrow ...

I daily confer with the best men before the House sits, and deliver out notes of directions, contrived by Mr Palmer and the ablest lawyers and perused by my Lord Southampton ... and the soberest statesmen, by which all with whom I had any correspondence, and many new men, direct their votes. I speak seldom, taking to myself and giving this maxim, that if any of our enemies or half friends move anything desired in my notes, that it be presently seconded and brought to the question, our number being much superior.

[Monk] did yesterday declare himself to Geoffrey Palmer as entirely the king's as any subject of his in the three kingdoms; but privately to him and this day publicly in the House he declared himself bound in honour and by his word to see all sales confirmed to the soldiers ...

Broderick to Hyde, 4 May 1660 (misdated the 13th), *Clarendon State Papers,* [6], vol. III, pp. 747–9.

DOCUMENT 13 THE BILL TO CONFIRM THE FUNDAMENTAL LAWS

Be it enacted ... that the Parliaments of England and the members thereof shall forever hereafter fully and freely enjoy all their ancient and just rights and privileges ... and ... that the Great Charter of the liberties of England ... chapters 5th, 14th and 29th, with all acts heretofore made for the confirmation and observation thereof; the statute made in the time of King Edward I, commonly called statutum de tallagio non concedendo, with all other statutes since made against any tax, tallage, aid, loan or other charge not set by common consent in Parliament; the Petition of Right ... with all the Acts therein recited ... together with the several Acts made [in 1641, concerning Star Chamber, High Commission, Ship Money, forest laws and knighthood fines] ... and all other statutes formerly made and unrepealed for the defence and preservation of the rights and privileges of Parliaments and their members, the lives, liberties, freeholds and properties of the subjects, against arbitrary and illegal taxes shall be and are hereby confirmed and shall be from henceforth forever inviolably observed ... and that His Majesty himself and all his officers ... and all his royal successors and their public officers shall take a personal oath duly to maintain, observe and execute   all and every the said laws and statutes to the best of their power ...

House of Lords Record Office, Parchment Collection, Box 12, Bill for the Confirmation of the Privileges of Parliament, 3 July 1660.

DOCUMENT 14   DEBATES ON THE CHURCH, JULY 1660

These extracts from debates on a bill 'for the maintenance of the true reformed Protestant religion' show the positions of Anglicans and Presbyterians on doctrine and church government and the efforts of court spokesmen to shelve the matter.

Mr Throgmorton said he would not be for the Presbyterian government because he had taken the oaths of allegiance and supremacy and urged how Knox and Buchanan had written against kings if they governed not well, and said, no bishop, no king ...

Moved by Sir Trevor Williams to establish the religion according to the Thirty-nine Articles and not only according to the Old and New Testaments [as the bill proposed] which all that own Christianity profess ...

Mr Prynne said he reverenced the Thirty-nine Articles but thought it unnecessary to insert them in this bill ...

Sir Heneage Finch said not one letter of the bill made good the title, saying the religion of our Church is not to seek, but we have enjoyed it long and therefore now should not be to enquire for it, but moved that it be referred to an assembly of divines, for which we ought to petition the king, and said there was no law to alter the government of the Church by bishops ... [He spoke] again against the paragraph and particularly liberty to tender consciences, which he said no man knew what 'twas ...

Mr Bunckley thought a moderate episcopacy might take in the good of both parties and urged the king's present inclinations and endeavours and said that episcopacy was more boundless than monarchy as it was used, saying some of them gloried to put down all lectures in the country and 'twas a fault to preach twice a Sunday, but said that government by episcopacy, if circumscribed, was to be wished ...

Sir Anthony Cooper said our religion was too much intermixed with interest, neither was it ripe enough now to handle religion, but moved that the whole committee might be adjourned for three months and this debate laid aside ...

The committee sate an hour in the dark before candles were suffered and those were blown out twice, but the third time they were preserved, though with great disorder and then 'twas voted, about ten at night, that the king be desired to convene a select number of divines to treat concerning this debate and the committee not to sit until October next the twenty-third.

Diary of Seymour Bowman MP, Bodleian Library, MS Dep. f. 9, fos. 54, 62–6, 77–85 (debates of 6, 9 and 16 July: the final extract, though under the 9th, seems to belong to the 16th).

DOCUMENT 15   **THE WORCESTER HOUSE DECLARATION**

This contained the most extensive concessions offered to the Presbyterians.

No bishop shall ordain, or exercise any part of jurisdiction which appertains to the censures of the Church, without the advice and assistance, of the presbyters; and no ... officials, as such, shall exercise any act of spiritual jurisdiction in these cases, viz. excommunication, absolution, or wherein any of the ministry are concerned, with reference to their pastoral charge .... Nor shall the archdeacon exercise any jurisdiction without the advice and assistance of six ministers of his archdeaconry, whereof three to be nominated by the bishop and three by the election of the major part of the presbyters within the archdeaconry ... We will take care that confirmation be rightly and solemnly performed, by the information and with the consent of the minister of the place; who shall admit none to the Lord's supper till they have made a credible profession of their faith and promised obedience to the will of God ... and that all possible diligence be used for the instruction and reformation of scandalous offenders, whom the minister shall not suffer to partake of the Lord's table until they have openly declared themselves to have truly repented and amended their former naughty lives ...

   Though we do esteem the liturgy ... contained in the Book of Common Prayer ... to be the best we have seen ... yet since we find some exceptions made against several things therein, we will appoint an equal number of learned divines of both persuasions to review the same and to make such alterations as shall be thought most necessary ... and that it be left to the minister's choice to use one or other at his discretion ... In the meantime, out of compassion and compliance towards those who would forbear the cross in baptism, we are content that no man shall be compelled to use the same ... No man shall be compelled to bow at the name of Jesus ... without reproaching those who, out of their devotion, continue that ancient ceremony of the Church. For the use of the surplice we are contented that all men be left to their liberty to do as they shall think fit, without suffering in the least degree for wearing or not wearing it ...

Browning, [2], pp. 365–70.

DOCUMENT 16   THE ARMY, THE MILITIA AND TAXATION

Here Andrew Marvell tells the mayor and corporation of Hull of events in Parliament, stressing that disbanding the army takes priority even over reducing taxation.

We have made a vote for bringing in an Act of a new assessment for six months of £70,000 per mensem to begin next January. The truth is the delay ere moneys can be got in eats up a great part of all that is levying ... And that is all that can be said for excuse of ourselves to the country, to whom we had given our own hopes of no further assessment to be raised ... it will be each man's ingenuity not to grudge an after-payment for that settlement and freedom from armies and navies which before he would have been glad to purchase with his whole fortune ... there being so great a provision made for money I doubt not but ere we rise to see the whole army disbanded and, according to the Act, hope to see your town once more ungarrisoned ... I cannot but remember, though then a child, those blessed days when the youth of your own town were trained for your militia, and did, methought, become their arms much better than any soldiers that I have seen there since ...

Marvell, [21], vol. II, pp. 1–2.

DOCUMENT 17   THE ACCUSATIONS AGAINST CLARENDON

Here an official at the French embassy sets out the claim, current in the queen's circle, that Clarendon had deliberately failed to enhance the king's powers, a claim based on a gross exaggeration of the monarchy's strength in 1660.

The chancellor believes the world is well governed when England is quiet; ... he wishes [the king] to be a good Englishman and nothing more ... He has always been against putting on foot the guards which the king has raised, no matter how evident the danger might be ... This man does not understand the importance of that sort of power, especially for a king of England; also during these recent conspiracies he advised the king to disband General Monk's regiment, which was the last remaining of the army ... He intended that the king should be guarded only by the affection and love of his subjects, who show four times a year that they do not know whether they love themselves ... Everything he does shows the same weak and lowly spirit, natural in a lawyer ...

When the king returned, he did so as master of everything. I beg you to ask the opinion of anyone well-informed – the queen understands this perfectly. He could have kept up an army of 6,000 men if he had wanted, everybody was at his feet, full of affection, being so weary of the severity of the last government ... He could have established whatever religion he wished, he could have changed the form of government without opposition, he could have taken off the penal laws from the Catholics ... Now, however, all this power has diminished, people have changed their minds, their ardour has been allowed to cool ... since the king has done no great things, the ill-intentioned have regained courage ... there remains a certain republican spirit among the generality of people ... which now is regaining strength, since the government has lacked the strength and the boldness to master it in a manner as absolute, authoritative and acknowledged as that seen in France ... Hyde wishes the law to govern, and so, to be accurate, he is more the minister of the law than of the prince ...

Bartet to Mazarin, 31 January–10 February 1661, Public Record Office, PRO 31/3/109, fos. 49, 256 (the latter part of the despatch is wrongly entered under 14–24 January).

DOCUMENT 18 **DISAGREEMENT ABOUT THE CORPORATION BILL**

The Commons' bill to remove the 'disaffected' from corporations was drastically amended by the Lords. The Commons here claim that the amendments would destroy municipal autonomy.

The second amendment strikes out all the commissioners' names and the powers given to remove ill members and restore those who were unjustly removed, to which we cannot agree, because
1. The whole regulation of corporations doth consist of placing the government in right hands; which by the bill sent up was put in a probable way of being effected, by this amendment is not so much as thought of; provision is made for nominating mayors and recorders, but no care for other members.
2. Nothing enacted by their lordships seems to us to provide for present safety ...
3. So total an alteration of the government may have an ill effect upon the free elections ...
4. No care taken that, if [charters are] renewed, they shall have their old privileges, nor for putting in good men.
5. The reformation in the bill sent up, but temporary ... These amendments would make a perpetual change; and we have no cause to believe it either so agreeable to the desires of the corporations for which we serve, or so consonant with our trust.
6. The intermeddling of justices of peace of the counties in corporate towns may occasion a clashing of jurisdictions and a disturbance of government ...

Commons Journals, [10], vol. VIII, p. 312.

DOCUMENT 19   COURT FACTION AND PARLIAMENTARY
TURBULENCE

*Daniel O'Neill describes the Commons' investigations into misgovernment in
1663 and blames them on court faction.*

We are falling into the courses of the old Long Parliament with a much
swifter pace than that did. Our purest Cavaliers are more troublesome and
malicious inspectors into the king and his ministers' behaviour than ever
Hampden or Pym were. Every day we have some mad bill brought in ...
The truth is, the disputes of the court have raised these spirits and their
reconciliations cannot allay them; nor do I believe any other charm will, but
that which I despair of, which is His Majesty's changing his present manner
of living and strongly applying his thoughts to his business, which is
governed little to the satisfaction of those that wish well to him or to the
peace of the kingdom.

Bodleian Library, Carte MS. 32, fo. 597.

DOCUMENT 20   CLARENDON SEEKS TO PROTECT THE
PRESBYTERIANS

*In February 1662 the Commons passed a bill which would have driven
Presbyterians out of livings in the Church of England, even before the
uniformity bill became law. Clarendon helped have the bill rejected by the
Lords, despite threats from some MPs to withhold money.*

At first all the bishops ... were against it and most of the Protestant lords
temporal. But my lord chancellor was resolved to oblige the Presbyterians
... and at last got seven of the bishops to join with him ... The Duke of
York was likewise brought over by his father-in-law and the Earl of Bristol
was vehement in the thing, and all the Popish lords. The Presbyterian
ministers sent Calamy, Baxter and Bates that day to the chancellor to give
him thanks. Some of the Commons going to the king the day before to
desire him to express himself positively against the confirmation of the
ministers, he said he had promised them at Breda the continuance of their
livings; whereupon they said the Commons might possibly, many of them,
be tempted not to pass the bill intended for the enlarging of his revenue if
His Majesty would favour the confirmation of the Presbyterian ministers; to
whom the king answered that if he had not wherewith to subsist two days,
he would trust God Almighty's providence, rather than break his word.

Rawdon Papers, [26], p. 138.

DOCUMENT 21　AN ATTEMPT TO AMEND THE
　　　　　　　UNIFORMITY BILL

This proviso, introduced in the Lords on the king's recommendation, was rejected by the Commons.

Provided always that, notwithstanding anything in this Act, in regard of the gracious offers and promises made by His Majesty before his happy Restoration of liberty to tender consciences ... as likewise the several services of those who contributed thereunto ... Be it therefore enacted that it shall and may be lawful for the king's majesty ... so far to dispense with any minister as upon 29 May 1660 was, and at present is, seised of any benefice ... and of whose merit towards His Majesty and of whose peaceable and pious disposition His Majesty shall be sufficiently informed and satisfied, that no such ministers shall be deprived ... for not wearing the surplice, or for not signing with the sign of the cross in baptism, so as he permit and bear the charge of some other licensed minister to perform that office towards such children whose parents shall desire the same, and so as such ministers shall not defame the liturgy, rites and ceremonies established in the Church of England ...

Historical Manuscripts Commission, 7th Report, Appendix, pp. 162–3.

DOCUMENT 22　ROYALIST POLITICAL IDEAS

These extracts are from the addresses to the Cheshire quarter sessions by Sir Peter Leicester, in 1670 and 1676.

Now whosoever will more diligently examine the beginning of things will find that nations did not originally spring up into kingdoms or commonwealths by the mutual consent of the people: for in the beginning ... all rule consisted in the heads of families, and in them the first born by succession, without any suffrages or election, as it were by a certain right of nature, was esteemed a prince of his whole kindred, both in sacred and civil matters, who chastised offenders at pleasure ... and in process of time paternal authority grew up into the name and power of kings ... Now as monarchy is the most natural form of government, so is it the most perfect and best form ... far above either aristocracy or democracy ...

　A good king or monarch that rules well (as, blessed be God, ours doth) will always take care for the good of his subjects and will observe the laws established and the rules of good government; and if a bad monarch succeed, who would break the laws, he is only punishable by God, to whom he must certainly one day render an account of all his actions; but he is not to be resisted by his subjects ... He that goes about to limit his prince cannot be a loyal subject; for that were to open a gap to rebellion; and if in one thing he may be resisted, then certainly in another: and so such subjects will be both judges and parties ... I have shown before that ... supreme power of government in monarchs and kings cannot be derived from the people: then it must needs follow that they have it from God: and then it is in the monarchy *iure divino* ...

Sir P.Leicester, *Charges to the Grand Jury at Quarter Sessions, 1660–77*, ed. E.M. Halcrow, Chetham Society, 1953, pp. 57–8, 77–8.

DOCUMENT 23   THE UNDERLYING STRENGTH OF MONARCHY

In about 1675 William III expressed a fear of a possible civil war in Engand; Sir William Temple, English ambassador at the Hague, told him that this was most unlikely.

I told him that the crown of England stood upon surer foundations than ever it had done in former times and the more for what had passed in the last reign, and that I believed the people would be found better subjects than perhaps the king himself believed them. That it was, however, in his power to be as well with them as he pleased, and to make as short turns to such an end; if not, yet with a little good husbandry he might pass his reign in peace, though not perhaps with so much ease at home or glory abroad as if he fell into the vein of his people.

Temple, [29], pp. 153–4.

DOCUMENT 24   BURNET ON CHARLES II

Gilbert Burnet included an assessment of Charles's character in his History of My Own Time, *published in the 1720s. This earlier version (c. 1683) is perhaps more revealing.*

He is very affable not only in public but in private, only he talks too much and runs out too long and too far; he has a very ill opinion both of men and women, and so is infinitely distrustful; he thinks the world is governed wholly by interest, and indeed he has known so much of the baseness of mankind that no wonder if he has hard thoughts of them; but when he is satisfied that his interests are likewise become the interests of his ministers, then he delivers himself up to them in all their humours and revenges ... He has often kept up differences amongst his ministers and has balanced his favours pretty equally amongst them ... he naturally inclines to refining and loves an intrigue ... He loves his ease so much that the great secret of all his ministers is to find out his temper exactly and to be easy to him. He has many odd opinions about religion and morality; he thinks an implicitness in religion is necessary for the safety of government and he looks upon all inquisitiveness into these things as mischievous to the state; he thinks all appetites are free and that God will never damn a man for allowing himself a little pleasure ... I believe he is no atheist, but that rather he has formed an odd idea of the goodness of God in his mind; he thinks to be wicked, and to design mischief, is the only thing that God hates ...

H. C. Foxcroft (ed.), *Supplement to Burnet's History of My Own Time*, Oxford, 1902, pp. 48–50.

DOCUMENT 25 HALIFAX ON CHARLES II

As a senior minister in Charles's last years, Halifax here writes from first-hand experience.

He lived with his ministers as he did with his mistresses; he used them, but he was not in love with them. He showed his judgment in this, that he cannot properly be said ever to have had a favourite, though some might look so at a distance ... he tied himself no more to them than they did to him, which implied a sufficient liberty on either side ...

He had back stairs to convey informations to him, as well as for other uses; and though such informations are sometimes dangerous (especially to a prince that will not take the pains necessary to digest them) yet in the main that humour of hearing everybody against anybody kept those about him in more awe than they would have been without it. I do not believe that ever he trusted any man or any set of men so entirely as not to have some secrets in which they had no share; as this might make him less well served, so in some degree it might make him the less imposed upon.

Halifax, [14], pp. 255–6.

DOCUMENT 26 COURT FACTION

Ruvigny was better informed than most French ambassadors, as a Protestant with numerous contacts outside the court.

The council consists of ministers with a mortal hatred of one another, who seek only to be avenged upon each other at the expense of their master's service; this means that there is great uncertainty in the resolutions which are taken ... [so] that one can never be sure of anything ...

The courtiers are normally attached to Parliament and, following the movements of that great body, they often allow themselves to be drawn along, against the interest of their master, for they know by experience that the most sure way to gain advancement is to make a great deal of noise, which obliges them always to urge the king to satisfy Parliament, hoping that that assembly will give money, of which they are sure to have the largest share.

Ruvigny to Louis XIV, 6–16 April 1674 and 29 March–8 April 1675, Public Record Office, PRO 31/3/131 and 31/3/132.

DOCUMENT 27   **THE KING REGAINS THE COMMONS' GOODWILL, 1670**

Marvell describes, with disapproval, how Charles won over a majority of MPs by backing the Commons in a dispute with the Lords and agreeing to a new conventicle bill.

All that interval [a two-month recess] there was great and numerous caballing among the courtiers. The king also all the while examined at council the reports from the commissioners of accounts, where they were continually discountenanced and treated rather as offenders than judges. In this posture we met, and the king, being extremely necessitous for money, ... told us the inconveniences which would fall on the nation by want of a supply should not lie at his door; that we must not revive any discord betwixt the Lords and us; that he himself had examined the accounts and found every penny to have been employed in the war ... When we began to talk of the Lords the king sent for us alone and recommended a rasure of all proceedings. The same thing ... that we proposed at first. We presently ordered it and went to tell him so ... At coming down (a pretty ridiculous thing!) Sir Thomas Clifford carried Speaker and Mace and all members there into the king's cellar, to drink his health. When the commissioners of accounts came before us, sometimes we heard them pro forma, but all falls to dirt ... [The Lords] are making mighty alterations in the conventicle bill (which, as we sent it up, is the quintessence of arbitrary malice) ... so the fate of the bill is uncertain, but must probably pass, being the price of money ...

Marvell, [21], vol. II, pp. 314–5.

DOCUMENT 28   **THE POLITICAL WATERSHED OF 1672**

Dering was one of many to see a major change in politics around 1672.

[After the Restoration] for twelve years more, we lived in peace, plenty and happiness above all nations of the world. But this blessing was too great to be continued long to those who deserved it so ill as we, and then the nation began to think the court inclined to favour Popery and France, grounding their suspicion upon

1. The declaration coming out about this time for laying aside all the penal laws in matters of religion.
2. The second war made with the Dutch in conjunction with France, there being no sufficient visible cause to provoke us to it.
3. The departing from the Triple League ...
4. The connivance at the Jesuits and priests, who did abundantly swarm in the kingdom and even about the court.
5. The conference between the king and his sister, Madame, the Duchess of Orleans, at Dover, the cause of meeting and the matter there debated and resolved on being kept very secret.
6. The employing of several known or suspected Papists in great places of trust, especially Lord Clifford, made High Treasurer.
7. Lastly to these, and much more than all these together, was the Duke of York's being first suspected and afterwards universally believed to be a Papist, which gave no unreasonable foundation to fear that, the king having no children, when the Duke should come to the crown the Protestant religion would be at least oppressed, if not extirpated.

Diaries and Papers of Sir Edward Dering, Second Baronet, ed. M. F. Bond, HMSO, 1976, pp. 125–6.

DOCUMENT 29   **DISCONTENT WITH, AND WITHIN, THE ARMY, 1673**

The anxiety about France and Popery was increased by the raising of extra forces for the war.

They say the soldiers were ready to mutiny at their decamping at Blackheath only upon a report of their uniting with the French army; everyone takes the liberty to talk what the Parliament will do next session, nay some ... say they wonder who durst print the articles of war, but that none dare put them in execution, and indeed they have not yet been proclaimed. They scruple the oath in it and say that to swear at large to obey the king's command is strange, for then he may command things [for] which the persons that do them shall afterwards be hanged ...

W. D. Christie (ed.), *Letters Addressed from London to Sir Joseph Williamson*, 2 vols, Camden Society, 1874, vol. I, p. 116.

DOCUMENT 30   **DANBY'S THOUGHTS ON POLICY, DECEMBER 1673**

Danby here sets out reasons why the Commons must be given the policies they want.

State of the present condition of the crown, which cannot be amended but by force or by compliance.

If by compliance, then it must be by Parliament or infinite reducement of expense.

If by Parliament, by this or a new one.

If by this, they must be gratified by executing the laws both against Popery and nonconformity and withdrawing apparently from the French interest.

If by a new one, they will either desire comprehension or toleration of all religions but Popery, and as to France the inclinations will be the same, only the new one will in all likelihood press the crown to it with less respect.

And, as to money, it is probably to be feared that neither the one nor the other will give anything proportionable to the wants of the crown till satisfied in their fears as to France ...

Browning, [41], vol. II, p. 63.

DOCUMENT 31   **TORY PROPAGANDA**

The Exclusionist Whigs relied heavily on anti-Popery, accusing the Tories of being crypto-Papists. Here a leading Tory pamphleteer counters that accusation and alleges that the Whigs wish to start another civil war.

A legal and effectual provision against the danger of Romish practices and errors will never serve their turn, whose quarrel is barely to the name of Popery, without understanding the thing itself. And if there were not a Roman Catholic left in the three kingdoms, they would be never the better satisfied, for where they cannot find Popery they will make it, nay, and be troubled too that they could not find it. It is no new thing for a popular outcry in the matter of religion to have a state faction in the belly of it. The first late clamour was against downright Popery, and then came on Popishly affected (that sweeps all). The order of bishops and the discipline of the Church took their turns next; and the next blow was at the crown itself; when every man was made a Papist that would not play the knave and the fool, for company, with the common people.

R. L'Estrange, *History of the Plot* (1679), Preface.

DOCUMENT 32   **A TORY MODERATE**

Roger North, in his life of his brother, Lord Keeper Guilford, argues that to stress royal authority and the subject's obedience was not to claim that the king was above the law.

His lordship was commonly reputed a high flier or prerogative man. It was true enough that his judgment was to give the crown all its lawful prerogatives; and he would willingly have consented that it should have had, in some cases, title to more ... But that he was not equally just to the people, in all their rights, as well of form as of substance, is utterly false. If we justly regard his censurers it will be found that his chief blame ... was only that he would not sacrifice the law to the iniquity of the times ... while he was of the opinion that the Tory party, in the temper of those times, pursued the true interest of England, that is to support the Church and crown according to the legal establishment of both, he was a Tory as they called it. But when the Tory party, or rather some pretended leaders, exceeded in joining with such as exalted the power of the crown above the law and sought to pull down the Church; then he was dropped from the Tory list and turned Trimmer.

R. North, *Lives of the Norths*, ed. E. Jessopp, 3 vols, Bell, 1890, vol. I, p. 249.

DOCUMENT 33   **WHIG POLITICAL ARGUMENT**

Much Whig propaganda was crude anti-Popery; this passage attempts a rational political argument, although the logic and history are both somewhat shaky.

The representative of the people, the Commons, whose business it is to present all grievances, as they are most likely to observe soonest the folly and treachery of those public servants ... so this representation ought to have no little weight with the prince ... The best of our princes have with thanks acknowledged the care and duty of their Parliaments in telling them of the corruption and folly of their favourites. Edward I, Henry II, Henry IV, Henry V and Queen Elizabeth never failed to do it, and no names are remembered with greater honour in English annals. Whilst the disorderly, the troublesome and the unfortunate reigns of Henry III, Edward II, Richard II and Henry VI ought to serve as landmarks to warn succeeding kings from preferring secret counsels to the wisdom of their Parliaments.

Quoted in B. Behrens, 'The Whig theory of the Constitution in the Reign of Charles II', *Cambridge Historical Journal*, vol. VII, 1941, p. 59.

DOCUMENT 34   **THE RESILIENCE OF URBAN DISSENT**

This letter describes how Dissenters re-established themselves in Great Yarmouth corporation after the 1662 purge.

Between 1662 and 1666 [all but two of the bailiffs and justices] ever stood for the king and Church's interest in the late unhappy times, and in all the foregoing years the laws against Nonconformists were so effectually executed that not a conventicle was to be seen in the town but, if discovered, was immediately prosecuted. But in '66 when Mr Thaxter ... and Capt. Huntington came to be bailiffs and Sir George England ... a justice, the scale was turned, the Nonconformists then publicly met and not the least check on them ... if you peruse the address to Richard Protector, you will find those chiefly concerned in it to have the greatest share in the government of this town from '65 to the present day, from whence the Nonconformists here took courage to contemn both the laws and the king's commands and to grow so numerous as they are.

Calendar of State Papers Domestic, [4] 1676–7, pp. 221–2.

DOCUMENT 35   **THE COMPTON CENSUS, 1676**

Designed to show that conformists heavily outnumbered Dissenters and Catholics, the census covered the province of Canterbury: the figures for that of York were assumed to be one-sixth those for Canterbury. The account of the province of Canterbury was by Archdeacon Samuel Parker.

	Conformists	Nonconformists	Papists
Province of Canterbury	2,123,362	93,151	11,878
Province of York	353,892	15,525	1,978
	2,477,254	108,676	13,856

AN ACCOUNT OF THE PROVINCE OF CANTERBURY

In taking these accounts we find these things observable:
1. That many left the Church upon the late [Declaration of] indulgence who before did frequent it.
2. Sending for the present enquiries has caused many to frequent the Church ...
3. That the Presbyterians are divided. Some of them come sometimes to church; therefore such are not wholly Dissenters ...
4. A considerable part of Dissenters are not of any sect whatsoever.
5. Of those who come to church, very many do not receive the sacrament ...

Calendar of State Papers Domestic, [4] 1693, pp. 448–50.

DOCUMENT 36   THE NATURE OF NONCONFORMITY

These letters from the parsons of Adderbury and Over Worton were in answer to a questionnaire on Dissent in the diocese of Oxford in 1682. The second parish is more typical than the first.

Besides that indifferency and coldness in religion, and that worldly-mindedness which possesses the generality, we have a factious schismatical spirit which reigns amongst us; we have two fruitful nurseries unfortunately placed amongst us, one Quakers, the other Presbyterian.

As for the Quakers, I acknowledge my unsuccessfulness, notwithstanding my endeavours ... for Bray Doyly, who is the ring-leader and lord of one part of the manor, upon any vacancy in it fills it with Quakers from other parts and, it seems, resolves to admit no tenants but such. They keep a constant meeting Sundays and Wednesdays in a house built upon his estate for that purpose.

The Presbyterians, about a little mile from the town, they keep a conventicle, peopled from all quarters round about ... This has a very ill influence ... especially upon this parish, for though we have very few indeed that wilfully and constantly absent themselves from the offices of the Church ... yet they, many of them, will straggle one part of the day thither, when they duly attend the public worship of God on the other, and they seem to be like the borderers betwixt two kingdoms, one can't well tell what prince they are subject to. This ... has been my great trouble, but unfortunately, living under a slack magistracy, has been out of my power to redress ...

The Dissenters in my parish of Over Worton ... are five women in four distinct families, persons of inferior rank, little sense and, I hope, no bad influence, they seeming weary of their ways and (as many others already) only ashamed to return. Two have been anciently Quakers, a third owns and pleads for that sect, but there is hopes of her return, the fourth was bred an Independent, but these follow no meetings and their only pretext is the viciousness of others. The other hath sometimes frequented the Anabaptist meetings, since the late times of Indulgence ... Three of the Quakers' children I baptised upon my first coming thither, who continue of good report in our Church ...

M. Clapinson (ed.), *Bishop Fell and Nonconformity: Visitation Documents from the Oxford Diocese, 1682–3*, Oxfordshire Record Society, 1980, pp. 1–2, 32.

DOCUMENT 37   IGNORANCE OF RELIGION

This anecdote is taken from the papers of Oliver Heywood, a Yorkshire Presbyterian minister, and shows how some remote areas remained largely untouched by organised religion.

On November 4 1681 as I travelled towards Wakefield, about Hardger Moor I met with a boy, who would needs be talking. I begun to ask him some questions about the principles of religion; he could not tell me how many gods there be, nor persons in the godhead, nor who made the world, nor anything about Jesus Christ, or heaven or hell, or eternity after this life, nor for what end he came into the world, nor what condition he was born in. I asked him whether he thought he was a sinner, he told me he hoped not, yet this was a witty boy and could talk of any worldly things skilfully enough... He is ten years of age, cannot read and scarce ever goes to church. His name is Thomas Brook, his parents died when he was a child.

Oliver Heywood, *Autobiography, Diaries, Anecdote and Event Books,* ed. J. Horsfall Turner, 4 vols, A.B. Bayes, Brighouse and T. Harrison, Bingley, 1882–5, vol. IV, p. 24.

DOCUMENT 38   MATHEMATICS AND PROGRESS

John Arbuthnot stresses the potential contribution of statistics, or political arithmetic, to human progress, while admitting that they are not yet being used as they should be.

Arithmetic is not only the great instrument of private commerce, but by it are (or ought to be) kept the public accounts of a nation; I mean, those that regard the whole state of a commonwealth, as to the number, fructification of its people, increase of stock, improvement of lands and manufactures, balance of trade, public revenues, coinage, military power by sea and land, etc. Those that would judge or reason truly about the state of any nation must go that way to work, subject all the forementioned particulars to calculation. That is the true political knowledge ... It is true [of some writers that] for want of good information their calculations sometimes proceed upon erroneous suppositions; but that is not the fault of the art. But what is it the government could not perform in this way, who have the command of all the public records?

Clark, [45], p. 141.

DOCUMENT 39   DECLINE OF THE BELIEF IN WITCHES

In this letter from Exeter in 1682, Lord Chief Justice North, later Lord Guilford, described the judges' embarrassment at having to enforce the laws against witchcraft, even though they doubted its existence.

Here have been three old women condemned for witchcraft ... I shall only tell you what I had from my brother [colleague] Raymond, before whom they were tried, that they were the most old, decrepit, despicable, miserable creatures that ever he saw. A painter would have chosen them out of the whole country for figures of that kind to have drawn by. The evidence against them was very full and fanciful, but their own confessions exceeded it. They appeared not only weary of their lives but to have a great deal of skill to convict themselves. Their descriptions of the sucking devils with saucer eyes were so natural that the jury could not choose but believe them. I find the country so fully possessed against them that, though some of the virtuosi may think these things the effects of confederacy, melancholy or delusion ... yet we cannot reprieve them without appearing to deny the very being of witches which, as it is contrary to law, so I think it would be ill for His Majesty's service, for it may give the faction occasion to set afoot the old trade of witch-finding, that may cost many innocent persons their lives, which this justice will prevent.

Calendar of State Papers Domestic, [4] 1682, p. 347.

CHRONOLOGY

THE RESTORATION SETTLEMENT

1660

1 January	Monk's army enters England.
21 February	'Secluded' MPs reinstated.
16 March	Long Parliament dissolves itself.
25 April	Convention meets.
29 May	Charles II enters London.
29 August	King assents to indemnity bill and bill to confirm judicial proceedings.
4 September	Commons agree to supply king with revenue of £1,200,000 a year.
25 October	Worcester House Declaration.
29 December	Convention dissolved.

1661

7 January	Venner's (Fifth Monarchist) rising.
8 May	Cavalier Parliament meets.
17 May	Commons order burning of Covenant.
June	Bill to secure the king's person and government passed, annulling all legislation which has not received the royal assent.
July	Bill passed declaring sole right to command of the militia and armed forces lies with the king; also Act against tumultuous petitioning.
December	Corporation bill passed.

1662

May	Act of Uniformity, Act against Quakers and Licensing Act passed.
August	Privy council rejects Presbyterian petition to dispense with parts of the Uniformity bill; ejections of clergy begin.

December	Bennet replaces Nicholas as secretary of state; the king issues his declaration in favour of toleration.
1663	
February	Commons refuse to consider any proposals to alter the Act of Uniformity.

THE REIGN OF CHARLES II

1663	Parliament is rent by faction, stemming from divisions at court.
	Bristol attempts to impeach Clarendon.
	'Northern rebellion' discovered.
1664	Triennial Act passed, replacing that of 1641.
	First Conventicle Act passed.
	Commons vote £2,500,000 for a war against the Dutch.
1665	Dutch War begins.
	Five Mile Act passed (to prevent non-conformist preachers living in corporate towns).
	Major outbreak of plague.
1666	Great Fire of London.
	Growing disillusionment with handling of Dutch War.
1667	Dutch fleet burns English ships in the Medway.
	Louis XIV invades Spanish Netherlands; Dutch make peace with England (Treaty of Breda).
	Fall of Clarendon; accounts committee appointed by Parliament to investigate mismanagement of Dutch War.
1668	Triple Alliance signed (England, the Dutch Republic and Sweden).
	First Conventicle Act lapses.
1669	Charles begins negotiations with Louis XIV for an alliance based on declaring himself a Catholic.

1670	Rapprochement between king and Commons: the king agrees to a new Conventicle Act as 'the price of money'. Secret Treaty of Dover signed. Widespread opposition to the implementation of the Conventicle Act.
1671	Continued good relations between king and Commons. Commons vote money after the king warns of the danger from France.
1672	Stop of the Exchequer (to provide ready money for the Dutch War). Charles and Louis declare war on the Dutch. Declaration of Indulgence. Duke of York fails to take Communion at Easter. French forces overrun five of the seven Dutch provinces; the English navy fails to gain mastery at sea. An army is raised for the war, but remains in England.
1673	Parliament recalled after more than a year: the king agrees to withdraw the Declaration of Indulgence and to pass the Test Act (to exclude Catholics from office) in return for money. York and Clifford resign their offices, rather than take the Test. The English navy still cannot gain supremacy at sea; the army remains in England. York marries a Catholic: the Commons urge the king not to allow the marriage to be consummated.
1674	Denied money by Parliament, Charles makes peace with the Dutch (Treaty of Westminster). 'Cabal' ministry finally breaks up: Danby (Lord Treasurer) becomes the kings's leading minister.
1675	Danby seeks the support of the bishops and endeavours to commit Charles to a firmly Anglican religious policy.

	'Danby's test', designed to confine office-holding to Anglicans: narrowly approved by the Lords, not presented to the Commons. Growing evidence in by-elections of political polarization; Parliament prorogued for fifteen months.
1676	Compton Census.
1677	Growing alarm at French military success in the Netherlands.
	York's daughter Mary married to William of Orange.
	Charles agrees to present ultimatum to Louis XIV.
1678	Charles prepares for war against France: raises large army, much of which is sent to Flanders.
	Charles also seeks money from France in return for making peace.
	Louis agrees to make peace with the allies (Treaty of Nijmegen).
	Titus Oates reveals alleged Popish Plot: numerous Catholics executed.
	Danby falls from power; Cavalier Parliament prorogued.
1679	Cavalier Parliament dissolved; new Parliament called.
	Danby impeached: York sent into exile.
	First exclusion bill: Parliament dissolved.
	Licensing Act lapses and with it press censorship.
	A second general election called: Charles delays meeting Parliament.
	Campaign of petitions for Charles to allow Parliament to meet.
1680	Charles continues to delay meeting Parliament.
	Petitions countered by 'abhorrences', leading to coining of terms 'Whig' and 'Tory'.
	Second 'Exclusion' Parliament meets.
	Exclusion bill passes Commons, rejected by Lords.

1681	Second 'Exclusion' Parliament dissolved; general election again produces 'Whig' majority in Commons.
	Third 'Exclusion' Parliament meets at Oxford; dissolved after one week.
	Charles publishes his reasons for dissolution.
	Tory reaction begins: Whig JPs and militia officers removed.
	Persecution of Dissenters intensifies.
	Quo warranto ordered against London's charter.
1682	Tory sheriffs chosen in London: Shaftesbury goes into exile.
	First new borough charters issued.
	York returns from Scotland.
1683	Rye House Plot discovered: several executed.
	Homes of Whigs and Dissenters searched for arms.
	London's charter adjudged to be forfeited: City to be governed by commissioners appointed by the king.
1684	Pace of charter surrenders accelerates.
	First steps to ease persecution of Catholics.
1685	
6 February	Charles II dies.

GLOSSARY

Absolutism Authoritarian monarchy, like that of Louis XIV's France: see [51] and [98].

Advowson The right to nominate the clergyman of a parish, often owned by a layman.

Ancient constitution A view of the constitution in which its salient features – king, parliaments and laws, the powers of the king and the rights of the subject – were believed to date back beyond the memory of man. The constitution was said to enshrine the wisdom of innumerable generations; guidance on current questions should be sought from the past. This was a conservative view, but not a static one: change was possible, indeed necessary, provided the basic framework and principles were preserved.

Chapter The governing body of a cathedral, headed by a dean, which also administered the cathedral's landed property.

Committee In both Houses of Parliament, bills were (and are) read twice by the full House and then referred to a committee, which goes over the wording in detail before returning the revised version to the full House for the third reading.

Conventicle An unauthorised nonconformist meeting.

Convocation The clergy's equivalent of Parliament. The Upper House consisted of the bishops, the Lower House of elected representatives of the parish clergy

'Country' Used in opposition to 'court', to describe criticism of both the king's court and the government in general, and more particularly the abuse of power. The criticism had strong moralistic overtones, being directed against waste, mismanagement and above all corruption.

'Court' This is used, in a parliamentary context, to mean the king's ministers and their supporters.

Covenant Under the alliance with the Scots (Solemn League and Covenant, 1643) all MPs, office-holders and ministers were required to declare, on oath, that they would defend the Parliamentary cause and reform the Churches of England and Ireland 'according to the Word of God and the example of the best reformed churches', which clearly implied the abolition of episcopacy. At the Restoration many Presbyterians were reluctant to renounce or denounce something that they had sworn so solemnly. Municipal officers were also required to renounce the Covenant under the Corporation Act.

Deputy lieutenants Under the command of the lord lieutenant, these were responsible for organizing and, if need be, commanding a county's militia. They were drawn from the upper gentry.

Engagement A promise, imposed by the Rump in 1650, to be true and faithful to the Commonwealth, as established without a king or House of Lords.

Excise Whereas customs duties were levied on exported or (more often) imported goods, the excise fell mainly on a range of goods produced and consumed at home, notably beer and other alcoholic drinks.

Hearth tax A rough property tax: the more hearths one had in one's home, the richer one was likely to be. The poorest were exempt but it was still unpopular because the collectors, like those of the excise, could enter private houses in the course of their investigations. There was also uncertainty as to whether industrial hearths (for example bakers' ovens) were exempt.

High Commission The top ecclesiastical court which exercised the jurisdiction which the Crown had taken away from the pope at the Reformation. Always unpopular with Puritans, it was abolished in 1641.

Impositions Customs duties imposed without parliamentary consent. These provided a major part of the early Stuarts' revenue until they were abolished in 1641.

JPs (Justices of the Peace) Chosen mostly from among the gentry, they were the key figures in county government, acting as both magistrates and administrators.

Militia A citizen force, commanded by the lord lieutenant and deputy lieutenants and responsible for local defence. As Parliament and the law did not recognise the existence of a standing army, debates about the control of the militia also involved the issue of the control of the army and navy, all being taken away from Charles I in 1642 and restored to his son in 1661.

Parliamentarian This can mean a member of Parliament, but in this book it is always used to mean someone who took Parliament's side in the civil wars.

Presbyterian Used in a political sense to describe the more moderate Parliamentarians, it was more properly a religious term, used of those who wanted a Puritan established Church. Some Presbyterians were dogmatically opposed to bishops; many were prepared to accept them, provided their powers were limited. All disliked the ceremonies practised in the Church of England on one hand and the excesses of the sects on the other.

Puritan A much-used term which is difficult to define. It covers a wide spectrum of practice and opinion, but most Puritans shared a greater than average religious zeal, an active hostility to what they regarded as sin and a preference for a church service without ceremonies and with the emphasis on preaching.

Star Chamber An offshoot of the privy council, this was in Tudor times popular with litigants, because it dealt with cases quickly, cheaply and equitably. Under Charles I it became unpopular as an instrument of political and religious repression and it was abolished in 1641.

Tithes In theory, parishioners gave a tenth of the produce of their land for the maintenance of the parish clergyman. In practice, the sums they paid often became fixed, and in many parishes at least some of the tithes were impropriated – paid to someone other than the clergyman, often a layman.

Triennial Acts That of 1641 declared that Parliament should meet at least once every three years, for a minimum of fifty days, and laid down elaborate procedures to ensure that it would meet even if the king failed to summon it. The 1664 Act omitted both the minimum period of sitting and the machinery for Parliament to assemble without the king.

Wardship Many landowners' estates were technically held from the king under ancient feudal tenures, by which an heir had to make a payment to the king on succeeding his father (livery), while the king became the heir's guardian if he succeeded while under age; usually, in fact, the king would sell the right of guardianship to the heir's relatives. These tenures thus imposed an occasional, but sometimes severe, financial burden on landed families. They were abolished in 1660, but the king was compensated with half the excise.

BIBLIOGRAPHY

PRIMARY SOURCES

1 Baxter, R., *Reliquiae Baxterianae*, ed. M. Sylvester, London, 1696. [Abridged edition published as *The Autobiography of Richard Baxter*, ed. N. Keeble, Everyman Library.]

2 Browning, A. (ed.), *English Historical Documents, 1660–1714*, Eyre and Spottiswoode, 1953.

3 Burnet, G., *History of my own Time*, 6 vols, Oxford University Press, 1833.

4 *Calendar of State Papers, Domestic, Charles II*, 30 vols, HMSO, 1860–1938.

5 Clarendon, Earl of (E. Hyde), *Calendar of Clarendon State Papers*, eds W. D. Macray and F. J. Routledge, 5 vols, Oxford University Press, 1872–1970.

6 Clarendon, Earl of (E. Hyde), *Clarendon State Papers*, 3 vols, Oxford University Press, 1767–86.

7 Clarendon, Earl of (E. Hyde), *History of the Rebellion*, ed. W.D. Macray, 6 vols, Oxford University Press, 1888.

8 Clarendon, Earl of (E. Hyde), *The Life*, 3 vols, Oxford University Press, 1827.

9 *Clarke Papers*, vol. IV, ed. C.H. Firth, Camden Society, 1901.

10 *Commons Journals*, vols VII–IX.

11 Gardiner, S. R. (ed.), *Constitutional Documents of the Puritan Revolution, 1625–60*, 3rd edn, Oxford University Press, 1951.

12 Grey, A., *Debates in the House of Commons, 1667–94*, 10 vols, London, 1769.

13 Gumble, T., *Life of General Monk*, London, 1671.

14 Halifax, Marquis of (G. Savile), *Complete Works*, ed. J.P. Kenyon, Penguin, 1969.

15 *Historical Manuscripts Commission, 5th Report, Appendix*, Sutherland MSS, HMSO, 1876.

16 Kenyon, J. P., *The Stuart Constitution*, 2nd edn, Cambridge University Press, 1986.

17 Lister, T. H., *Life and Administration of Clarendon*, 3 vols, 1837–8 [vol. III consists of documents].

18 *Lords Journals*, vols XI–XIII.

19   Ludlow, E., *Memoirs*, ed. C.H. Firth, 2 vols, Oxford University Press, 1894.
20   Ludlow, E., *A Voyce from the Watch Tower*, ed. B. Worden, Camden Society, 1978.
21   Marvell, A., *Poems and Letters*, ed. H.M. Margoliouth, 3rd edn, 2 vols, Oxford University Press, 1971.
22   *Nicholas Papers*, ed. G. F. Warner, 4 vols, Camden Society, 1886–1920.
23   'Old Parliamentary History': *The Parliamentary or Constitutional History of England from the Earliest Times to the Restoration*, 23 vols, London, 1751–61.
24   Pepys, S., *Diary*, eds R.C. Latham and W. Matthews, 11 vols, Bell, 1971–83.
25   Price, J., 'The Mystery and Method of His Majesty's Happy Restoration' in F. Maseres ed., *Select Tracts Relating to the Civil Wars in England*, London, 1815.
26   *Rawdon Papers*, ed. E. Berwick, London, 1819.
27   Reresby, Sir J., *Memoirs,* ed. A. Browning, revised M. K. Geiter and W. A. Speck, Royal Historical Society, 1991.
28   Rugg, T., *Diurnal*, ed. W. L. Sachse, Camden Society, 1961.
29   Temple, Sir W., *Memoirs, 1672–9*, London, 1692.
30   Thirsk, J. and Cooper, J. P. (eds), *Seventeenth-Century Economic Documents*, Oxford University Press, 1972.
31   Whitelocke, B. , *Diary*, ed. R. Spalding, British Academy, 1990.
32   Whitelocke, B., *Memorials of the English Affairs*, 4 vols, Oxford University Press, 1853.

SECONDARY WORK

33   Abernathy, G. R., jnr, 'The English Presbyterians and the Stuart Restoration, 1648–63', *Transactions of the American Philosophical Society*, new series, vol. LV, 1965.
34   Aylmer, G. E. (ed.), *The Interregnum: The Quest for Settlement*, Macmillan, 1972.
35   Aylmer, G. E., *The State's Servants: the Civil Service of the English Republic*, Routledge and Kegan Paul, 1973.
36   Baugh, D., 'Maritime Strength and Atlantic Commerce' in L. Stone, ed., *An Imperial State at War: Britain from 1689–1815*, Routledge, 1994. [Much of this essay relates to the 1650s and 1660s.]
37   Bolam, C. G., Goring, J. J., Short, H. L. and Thomas, R., *The English Presbyterians*, Allen & Unwin, 1968.
38   Bosher, R. S., *The Making of the Restoration Settlement: The Influence of the Laudians*, Dacre Press, 1951.
39   Braddick, M. J., *The Nerves of State: Taxation and the Financing of the English State, 1558–1714*, Manchester University Press, 1996.

40 Braddick, M. J., *Parliamentary Taxation in Seventeenth-Century England*, Royal Historical Society, 1994.

41 Browning, A., *Thomas Osborne, Earl of Danby*, 3 vols, Jackson, 1951 [vols. II and III consist of documents].

42 Chandaman, C. D., *The English Public Revenue, 1660–88*, Oxford University Press, 1975.

43 Challinor, P. J., 'Restoration and Exclusion in the County of Cheshire', *Bulletin of the John Rylands Library*, vol. LXIV, 1982.

44 Childs, J., *The Army of Charles II*, Routledge and Kegan Paul, 1976.

45 Clark, G. N., *Science and Social Welfare in the Age of Newton*, 2nd edn, Oxford University Press, 1949.

46 Clark, R., 'Why was the Re-establishment of the Church of England Possible? Derbyshire: a Provincial Perspective', *Midland History*, vol. VIII, 1983.

47 Cliffe, J. T., *The Puritan Gentry Besieged, 1650–1700*, Routledge, 1993.

48 Clifton, R., *The Last Popular Rebellion: The Western Rising of 1685*, Temple Smith, 1984.

49 Coleby, A., *Central Government and the Localities: Hampshire 1649–89*, Cambridge University Press, 1987.

50 Coward, B., *The Stanleys, Lords Stanley and Earls of Derby, 1385–1672*, Chetham Society, 1983.

51 Daly, J., 'The Idea of Absolute Monarchy in Seventeenth-Century England', *Historical Journal*, vol. XXI, 1978.

52 Davies, G., *The Restoration of Charles II*, Oxford University Press, 1955.

53 Davies, J. D., *Gentlemen and Tarpaulins: The Officers and Men of the Restoration Navy*, Oxford University Press, 1991.

54 Davis, R., *A Commercial Revolution 1660–1760*, Historical Association, 1967.

55 Dowdell, E. G., *A Hundred Years of Quarter Sessions: The Government of Middlesex, 1660–1760*, Cambridge University Press, 1932.

56 Feiling, K. G., *History of the Tory Party, 1640–1714*, Oxford University Press, 1924.

57 Figgis, J.N., *The Divine Right of Kings*, Harper & Row, 1965.

58 Fletcher, A., *Reform in the Provinces: The Government of Stuart England*, Yale University Press, 1986.

59 Forster, G., 'Government in Provincial England under the later Stuarts', *Transactions of the Royal Historical Society*, 5th series, vol. XXXIII, 1983.

60 Glassey, L. K. J., *Politics and the Appointment of Justices of the Peace, 1675–1720*, Oxford University Press, 1979.

61 Goldie, M., 'John Locke and Anglican Royalism', *Political Studies*, vol. 31, 1983.

62 Goldie, M., 'The Theory of Religious Intolerance in Restoration

England', in O. P. Grell, J. I. Israel and N. Tyacke eds, *From Persecution to Toleration*, Oxford University Press, 1991.

63 Green, I. M., *The Re-establishment of the Church of England*, Oxford, 1978.

64 Habakkuk, H. J., 'The Land Settlement and the Restoration of Charles II', *Transactions of the Royal Historical Society*, 5th series, vol. XXVIII, 1978.

65 Haley, K. H. D., *The First Earl of Shaftesbury*, Oxford University Press, 1968.

66 Harris, T., *London Crowds in the Reign of Charles II*, Cambridge University Press, 1987.

67 Harris, T., *Politics under the Later Stuarts, 1660–1715*, Longman, 1993.

68 Harris, T., 'Was the Tory Reaction Popular? Attitudes of Londoners towards the Prosecution of Dissent, 1661–86', *London Journal*, vol. XIII, 1988.

69 Harris, T., Seaward, P. and Goldie, M. (eds), *The Politics of Religion in Restoration England*, Blackwell, 1990. [See particularly M. Goldie, 'Danby, the Bishops and the Whigs'.]

70 Havighurst, A. F., 'The Judiciary and Politics in the Reign of Charles II', *Law Quarterly Review*, vol. LXVI, 1950.

71 Henning, B. D. (ed.), *The History of Parliament: The House of Commons 1660–90*, 3 vols, Secker & Warburg, 1983.

72 Hill, C., *Some Intellectual Consequences of the English Revolution*, Weidenfeld & Nicolson, 1980.

73 Hirst, D., 'The Conciliatoriness of the Cavalier House of Commons Reconsidered', *Parliamentary History*, vol. VI, 1987.

74 Holmes, C., *Seventeenth-Century Lincolnshire*, History of Lincolnshire, vol. VII, 1980.

75 Horwitz, H., 'Protestant Reconciliation in the Exclusion Crisis', *Journal of Ecclesiastical History*, vol. XV, 1964.

76 Hunter, M., *Science and Society in Restoration England*, Cambridge University Press, 1981.

77 Hurwich, J. J., 'Dissent and Catholicism in English Society: A Study of Warwickshire, 1660–1720', *Journal of British Studies*, vol. XVI, 1976.

78 Hutton, R., *Charles II*, Oxford University Press, 1989.

79 Hutton, R., *The Restoration, 1658–67*, Oxford University Press, 1985.

80 Jenkins, G. H., *The Foundations of Modern Wales, 1642–1780*, Oxford University Press, 1987.

81 Jenkins, P., *The Making of a Ruling Class: The Glamorgan Gentry, 1640–1790*, Cambridge University Press, 1983.

82 Jones, J. R., *Charles II: Royal Politician*, Allen and Unwin, 1987.

83 Jones, J. R., *The First Whigs*, Oxford University Press, 1961.

84 Jones, J. R. (ed.), *Liberty Secured? Britain before and after the Revolution of 1688*, Stanford University Press, 1992.

85 Jones, J. R. (ed.), *The Restored Monarchy, 1660–88*, Macmillan, 1979.

86 Kenyon, J. P., *The Popish Plot*, Heinemann, 1972.

87 Kenyon, J. P., *Robert Spencer, Earl of Sunderland*, Longman, 1958.

88 Knights, M., *Politics and Opinion in Crisis, 1678–81*, Cambridge University Press, 1994.

89 Lacey, D. R., *Dissent and Parliamentary Politics in England, 1660–89*, Rutgers University Press, 1969.

90 Landau, N., *The Justices of the Peace 1679–1760*, California University Press, 1984.

91 Malcolm, J. L., 'Charles II and the Reconstruction of Royal Power', *Historical Journal*, vol. XXXV, 1992.

92 Marshall, A., *Intelligence and Espionage in the Reign of Charles II*, Cambridge University Press, 1994.

93 Miller, J., *Charles II*, Weidenfeld and Nicolson, 1991.

94 Miller, J., 'Charles II and his Parliaments', *Transactions of the Royal Historical Society*, 5th series, vol. XXXII, 1982.

95 Miller, J., 'The Crown and the Borough Charters in the Reign of Charles II', *English Historical Review*, vol. C, 1985.

96 Miller, J., *James II: A Study in Kingship*, Methuen, 1989.

97 Miller, J., *Popery and Politics in England, 1660–88*, Cambridge University Press, 1973.

98 Miller, J., 'The Potential for "Absolutism" in Later Stuart England', *History*, vol. LXIX, 1984.

99 Miller, J., 'Public Opinion in Charles II's England', *History*, vol. LXXX, 1995.

100 Morrill, J. S. (ed.), *Reactions to the English Civil War*, Macmillan, 1982.

101 Norrey, P. J., 'The Restoration Regime in Action: the Relationship between Central and Local Government in Dorset, Somerset and Wiltshire', *Historical Journal*, vol. XXXI, 1988.

102 O'Brien, P. K. and Hunt, P. A., 'The Rise of a Fiscal State in England, 1485–1815', *Historical Research*, vol. LXVI, 1993.

103 Ogg, D., *England in the Reign of Charles II*, 2nd edn, Oxford University Press, 1956.

104 Outhwaite, R. B., 'Dearth and Government Intervention in English Grain Markets, 1590–1700', *Economic History Review*, 2nd series, vol. XXXIV, 1981.

105 Pickavance, R. G., 'The English Boroughs and the King's Government: A Study of the Tory Reaction, 1681–5', unpublished D. Phil. thesis, Oxford, 1976.

106 Pincus, S. C. A., *Protestantism and Patriotism: Ideologies and the Making of English Foreign Policy 1650–68*, Cambridge University Press, 1996.

107 Plumb, J. H., *The Growth of Political Stability in England, 1675–1725*, Macmillan, 1967.

108 Pocock, J. G. A., *The Ancient Constitution and the Feudal Law*, 2nd edn, Cambridge University Press, 1987.

109 Pruett, J. H., *The Parish Clergy under the later Stuarts: The Leicestershire Experience*, Illinois University Press, 1978.

110 Roberts, C., *The Growth of Responsible Government in Stuart England*, Cambridge University Press, 1966.

111 Roberts, S, 'Public or Private? Revenge and Recovery at the Accession of Charles II', *Bulletin of the Institute of Historical Research*, vol. LIX, 1986.

112 Roberts, S., *Recovery and Restoration in an English County: Devon Local Administration 1646–70*, Exeter University Press, 1985.

113 Roseveare, H., *The Financial Revolution, 1660–1760*, Longman, 1991.

114 Scott, J., *Algernon Sidney and the Restoration Crisis, 1677–83*, Cambridge University Press, 1991.

115 Scott, J., 'Radicalism and Restoration: The Shape of the Stuart Experience', *Historical Journal*, vol. 31, 1988.

116 Seaward, P., *The Cavalier Parliament and the Reconstruction of the Old Regime, 1661–7*, Cambridge University Press, 1989.

117 Seaward, P., *The Restoration 1660–88*, Macmillan, 1991.

118 Slack, P., *Poverty and Policy in Tudor and Stuart England*, Longman, 1988.

119 Sommerville, C. J., *Popular Religion in Restoration England*, Florida University Press, 1977.

120 Spufford, M. (ed.), *The World of Rural Dissenters, 1520–1725*, Cambridge University Press, 1995.

121 Spurr, J., 'The Church of England, Comprehension and the Toleration Act of 1689', *English Historical Review*, vol. CIV, 1989.

122 Spurr, J., *The Restoration Church of England, 1646–89*, Yale University Press, 1991.

123 Styles, P., *Studies in Seventeenth-Century West Midlands History*, Roundwood Press, 1978.

124 Sykes, N., *From Sheldon to Secker*, Cambridge University Press, 1959.

125 Thirsk, J., 'The Restoration Land Settlement', *Journal of Modern History*, vol. XXVI, 1954.

126 Thomas, K., *Religion and the Decline of Magic*, Penguin, 1973.

127 Thomas, R., 'Comprehension and Indulgence', in G. F. Nuttall and 0. Chadwick eds, *From Uniformity to Unity*, SPCK, 1962.

128 Tomlinson, H., *Guns and Government: The Ordnance Office under the later Stuarts*, Royal Historical Society, 1979.

129 Watts, M., *The Dissenters from the Reformation to the French Revolution*, Oxford University Press, 1978.

130 Western, J. R., *The English Militia in the Eighteenth Century, 1660–1802*, Routledge & Kegan Paul, 1965.

131 Weston, C. C. and Greenberg, J. F., *Subjects and Sovereigns: The Grand Controversy over Legal Sovereignty in Stuart England*, Cambridge University Press, 1981.

132 Whiteman, A., *The Compton Census of 1676*, British Academy, 1986.

133 Whiteman, A., 'The Re-establishment of the Church of England', *Transactions of the Royal Historical Society*, 5th series, vol V, 1955.
134 Whiteman, A., 'The Restoration of the Church of England', in G. F. Nuttall and O. Chadwick eds, *From Uniformity to Unity*, SPCK, 1962.
135 Witcombe, D. T., *Charles II and the Cavalier House of Commons*, Manchester University Press, 1966.
136 Woolrych, A., 'The Cromwellian Protectorate: A Military Dictatorship?', *History*, LXXV, 1990.

ADDITIONAL REFERENCES

137 Fletcher, A., *The Outbreak of the English Civil War*.
138 Evelyn, J., *Diary*, ed. E.S. deBeer, vol. III.
139 Bodleian Library, MS Dep. f. 9, fo. 49.
140 Public Record Office, PRO 31/3/108, Montagu to Mazarin, 16/26 November, 1660.
141 Bodleian Library, Carte MS 47, fo. 45.
142 Howell, T. (ed.), *State Trials*, vol. V.
143 Sheffield, J., Duke of Buckingham, *Works*, vol. II.

INDEX